UPPER COLUMBIA
BASIN NETWORK

Upper Columbia Basin Network Science Communication Plan

Version 1.0

Natural Resource Report NPS/UCBN/NRR—2009/140

Jannis L. Jocius
National Park Service, Upper Columbia Basin Network
University of Idaho, Department of Fish and Wildlife
Moscow, ID 83844-1136

Lisa K. Garrett
National Park Service, Upper Columbia Basin Network
University of Idaho, Department of Fish and Wildlife
Moscow, ID 83844-1136

August 2009

U.S. Department of the Interior
National Park Service
Natural Resource Program Center
Fort Collins, Colorado

The National Park Service, Natural Resource Program Center publishes a range of reports that address natural resource topics of interest and applicability to a broad audience in the National Park Service and others in natural resource management, including scientists, conservation and environmental constituencies, and the public.

The Natural Resource Report Series is used to disseminate high-priority, current natural resource management information with managerial application. The series targets a general, diverse audience, and may contain NPS policy considerations or address sensitive issues of management applicability.

All manuscripts in the series receive the appropriate level of peer review to ensure that the information is scientifically credible, technically accurate, appropriately written for the intended audience, and designed and published in a professional manner. This report received formal peer review by subject-matter experts who were not directly involved in the collection, analysis, or reporting of the data, and whose background and expertise put them on par technically and scientifically with the authors of the information.

Views, statements, findings, conclusions, recommendations, and data in this report are those of the author(s) and do not necessarily reflect views and policies of the National Park Service, U.S. Department of the Interior. Mention of trade names or commercial products does not constitute endorsement or recommendation for use by the National Park Service.

This report is available from the Upper Columbia Basin Network website (http://www.nature.nps.gov/im/units/UCBN) and the Natural Resource Publications Management website (http://www.nature.nps.gov/publications/NRPM).

Please cite this publication as:

Jocius, J. L., and L. K. Garrett. 2009. Upper Columbia Basin Network science communication plan: Version 1.0. Natural Resource Report NPS/UCBN/NRR—2009/140. National Park Service, Fort Collins, Colorado.

NPS 963/100250, August 2009

Change History

1. Version numbers increase incrementally by tenths (e.g., version 1.1, version 1.2, ...etc) for minor changes. Major revisions should be designated with the next whole number (e.g., version 2.0, 3.0, 4.0 ...etc.). Record the previous version number, date of revision, author of the revision, identify paragraphs and pages where changes are made, and the reason for making the changes along with the new version number.

2. Notify the UCBN Data Manager of any changes to the Communication Plan.

3. Post new versions on the Internet and forward copies to all individuals with a previous version of the Communication Plan. A list of recipients will be maintained in Appendix E at the end of this document.

Version #	Date	Revised by	Changes	Justification

Contents

Contents (continued)

Figures

Figures (continued)

Tables

Appendixes

Executive Summary

The mission of the National Park Service is "to conserve unimpaired the natural and cultural resources and values of the national park system for the enjoyment of this and future generations" (NPS 1999). To uphold this goal, the Director of the NPS approved the Natural Resource Challenge to encourage national parks to focus on the preservation of the nation's natural heritage through science, natural resource inventories, and expanded resource monitoring (NPS 1999). Through the Challenge, 270 parks in the national park system were organized into 32 inventory and monitoring networks.

Parks of the Upper Columbia Basin Network (UCBN) include: Big Hole National Battlefield, City of Rocks National Reserve, Craters of the Moon National Monument and Preserve, Hagerman Fossil Beds National Monument, John Day Fossil Beds National Monument, Lake Roosevelt National Recreation Area, Minidoka Internment National Monument, Nez Perce National Historical Park, and Whitman Mission National Historic Site.

The UCBN vital signs monitoring plan, finalized in July 2007, was developed over the course of four years. The monitoring plan identified 14 priority vital signs, indicators of ecosystem health, which represent a broad suite of ecological phenomena operating across multiple temporal and spatial scales. Each UCBN vital sign is addressed in a stand-alone peer-reviewed monitoring protocol that serves as a detailed study plan with step-by-step instructions for all participants involved in monitoring, from field technicians to data analysts and project leaders.

The UCBN recognizes the need to raise overall awareness about the work of the inventory and monitoring (I&M) program, the network's role and activities in I&M, and sharing monitoring status and trend results. Effective communication and outreach is a critical link in dissemination of I&M results. The success of the I&M program ultimately depends on whether park managers find the information produced by the UCBN to be useful in the management of natural resources in their park. In addition, to achieve that success, it is critical that park staff make their needs known to the UCBN.

This comprehensive science communications plan addresses the need to raise awareness and inform internal and external audiences of the UCBN's scientific findings. This plan also reiterates the importance of a two-way exchange of knowledge between the I&M program and the parks that they serve. Essentially, this plan details the why, where, how, and when of the UCBN's science communications program.

We have included descriptions of UCBN communication products such as resource briefs, informational posters, and a copy of our biannual newsletter. Our hope is that this communication plan will enable park staff to gain an understanding of the depth and breadth of the UCBN commitment to science communication. The intent of this plan is to ensure that a seamless and credible story about UCBN inventory and monitoring efforts is told to park managers and visitors.

Acknowledgements

Funding for this project was provided through the National Park Service Natural Resource Challenge and the Servicewide Inventory and Monitoring Program. We thank the authors of the Heartland Network and the Pacific Islands Network communication plans for allowing us to use and reference their network communication plans (CSU 2007; Haysmith and Nash 2009). We thank the superintendents, resource managers, and interpretive staffs from the Upper Columbia Basin Network Parks for their constructive reviews of earlier versions of this plan and participation in a communication needs assessment survey that assisted us in the development of this communication plan. We especially thank Jason Lyon from Nez Perce National Historical Park for reviewing the plan thoroughly and for supporting collaboration between the parks and the I&M program.

Introduction

The National Park Service (NPS) is required to use the highest quality science information to manage park resources (NPS 1999). Each year the Upper Columbia Basin Network (UCBN) Inventory and Monitoring (I&M) program collects, analyzes, interprets, and reports monitoring data to assist natural resource managers in gaining a better understanding of the status and trend of natural resources within their parks. These data and reports are used to assess the condition of natural resources and to inform management decisions. The UCBN I&M program is fundamentally an information system in which I&M data are analyzed, interpreted, and communicated to a diverse audience consisting of park managers and superintendents, peer scientists, and the lay public (Garrett et al. 2007).

The UCBN vital signs monitoring plan, finalized in July 2007, was developed over the course of four years. The monitoring plan identifies a suite of 14 vital signs chosen for monitoring implementation in UCBN parks (Table 1). Vital signs are "a subset of physical, chemical, and biological elements and processes of park ecosystems selected to represent the overall condition of park resources, known or hypothesized effects of stressors, or elements that have important human values" (Garrett et al. 2007). Each UCBN vital sign is addressed in a stand-alone peer-reviewed monitoring protocol that serves as a detailed study plan with step-by-step instructions for all participants involved in monitoring, from field technicians to data analysts and project leaders. UCBN staff and their cooperators make hundreds of observations each year about water quality, plant, and animal populations, communities, and park environments. This requires a commitment to comprehensive data management, reporting, and communication with parks.

Reporting is the process through which the UCBN derive information from the underlying data through analysis and interpretation for use by park managers. Some examples of vital signs monitoring reports are: 1) annual summaries written for park managers; 2) 5-year trend reports for park superintendents and managers; 3) internet websites for NPS staff and the general public; and 4) email bulletins for park superintendents, managers, and the general public. A well-developed UCBN communication strategy, with a written plan for guidance, will help ensure that the monitoring data collected will be reported to parks in a useful and informative format.

Lewis (2007) mentions that "one of the challenges faced by scientists is translating discoveries into procedures and practices that can be implemented by resource managers. To be relevant to managers, scientists should always ask themselves: How can resource managers use the information that [is being discovered]." Based on this, it is important to consider some key characteristics when communicating scientific information:

- **Use plain language.** If someone outside a scientist's area of expertise is not likely to understand a word, he/she should explain it or choose a different word.
- **Use pictures. They're worth a thousand words.** Sometimes people just need to see the information. This does not mean charts and graphs. Real pictures, or at least explanatory graphics that depict a situation, are always helpful.
- **Be short. Synthesize.** Information should be explained in 4-5 bullets. It is harder to work to boil things down to a few bullets than it is to tell the "rest of the story," however, by doing the work, the rewards, as far as communication goes, will be great (Lewis 2007).

UCBN staff recognizes the need to raise overall awareness about the I&M Program, the network's role and activities in I&M, and the importance of sharing inventory and monitoring results to a wide variety of audiences. Ultimately, the success of the UCBN I&M program will be judged by whether the scientific information produced was deemed useful in the management of park resources.

This plan is designed to address the why, where, how, and when of the UCBN's science communications program. We have included descriptions of communication products that have already been developed and some that are identified as future projects. This plan incorporates comments and suggestions made by park staff that assisted us in determining communication needs.

Since the UCBN works with a broad group of collaborators, we acknowledge that for monitoring information to be effective, analyses and interpretation needs to be provided at regular intervals and in formats specific to intended audiences. Reporting frequency, format, and the roles and responsibilities of UCBN staff and cooperators are described in this plan along with the UCBN commitment to delivering quality, meaningful monitoring information in a timely manner to diverse audiences.

Table 1. UCBN vital signs and measures in the Vital Signs framework developed by the NPS Vital Signs Monitoring Program.

Level 1 – Landscapes	Level 2 – Landscape Dynamics	Level 3 – Vital Sign	UCBN Vital Sign Name	Measures Collected	BIHO	CIRO	CRMO	HAFO	JODA	LARO	MIIN	NEPE	WHMI
Geology and soils	Geomorphology	Stream/river channel characteristics	Stream/river channel characteristics	Bankfull width and depth, substrate composition, bank angle, undercut depth, pool depth, and sinuosity.	X	X	X		X			X	X
Water	Hydrology	Surface water dynamics	Surface water dynamics	Flow rate and annual water level fluctuation.	X	X	X		X			X	X
	Water quality	Water chemistry	Water chemistry	Daily, seasonal and annual values for core parameters.	X	X	X		X			X	X
		Aquatic macroinvertebrates	Aquatic macroinvertebrates	Species and functional group composition and abundance (counts).	X	X	X		X			X	X
Biological integrity	Invasive species	Invasive/exotic plants	Invasive/exotic plants	Frequency (presence/absence), distribution, abundance (cover), detection of new species, and incipient invasions	X	X	X	X	X	X		X	X
	Focal species or communities	Riparian communities	Riparian vegetation	Abundance (cover) of target genera and species and strata, and composition of communities and community types.	X	X	X	X	X	X		X	X
		Shrubland communities	Sagebrush-steppe vegetation	Abundance (cover) of target species and genera and strata, tree density, composition, and diversity.		X	X	X	X	X			
		Forest/woodland communities	Aspen	Abundance (aspen stem density, conifer density), and tree height.		X	X						

3

Table 1. UCBN vital signs and measures in the Vital Signs framework developed by the NPS Vital Signs Monitoring Program (continued).

Level 1 - Landscapes	Level 2 – Landscape Dynamics	Level 3 - Vital Sign	UCBN Vital Sign Name	Measures Collected	BIHO	CIRO	CRMO	HAFO	JODA	LARO	MIIN	NEPE	WHMI
Biological integrity	Focal species or communities	Forest/woodland Communities	Limber pine	Frequency of trees infected, distribution of infection in parks, number and location of cankers and rate of survival after blister rust infection		X	X						
		Birds	Osprey	Nest occupancy (proportion occupied), productivity (fledglings per nest)						X			
		Birds	Sage grouse	Peak occupancy, abundance, distribution and amount of critical habitat, occupancy and abundance in critical habitat		X	X						
		Mammals	Bats	Riparian occupancy, cave occupancy and abundance, local extinction rates		X	X		X				
Human use	Cultural landscapes	Cultural landscapes	Camas lily	Abundance (density), flowering rate, frequency of target invasive plants	X							X	
Ecosystem pattern and processes	Land dynamics	Land cover and use	Land cover and use	Patch metric measures of connectivity and fragmentation, core areas, and areal coverage of general habitat types; housing density and road density; and measures of patterns of land ownership and management.	X	X	X	X	X	X	X		X

UCBN Inventory and Monitoring Program

The Natural Resource Challenge, approved by the Director of the National Park Service in 1999, directs parks to focus on the preservation of the nation's natural heritage through science, natural resource inventories and expanded resource monitoring (NPS 1999). Indeed, the mission of the NPS is "to conserve unimpaired the natural and cultural resources and values of the national park system for the enjoyment of this and future generations" (NPS 1999).

The single biggest undertaking of the Challenge was to augment ongoing park inventory and monitoring efforts into an ambitious comprehensive nationwide program. The servicewide Inventory and Monitoring (I&M) program was introduced to 270 parks identified as having significant natural resources. Under this program, parks were organized into 32 networks based on similar geographic and natural resource characteristics, allowing for improved efficiency and sharing of staff and resources. The network organization facilitates collaboration, information sharing, and economies of scale in natural resource monitoring. Networks are guided by a Board of Directors who specifies desired outcomes, evaluates performance for the monitoring program, and promotes accountability.

The primary goals of the I&M Program are to:

- Inventory the natural resources under National Park Service stewardship to determine their nature and status.
- Monitor park ecosystems to better understand their dynamic nature and condition and to provide reference points for comparisons with other, altered environments.
- Establish natural resource inventory and monitoring as a standard practice throughout the National Park system that transcends traditional program, activity, and funding boundaries.
- Integrate natural resource inventory and monitoring information into National Park Service planning, management, and decision making.
- Share National Park Service accomplishments and information with other natural resource organizations and form partnerships for attaining common goals and objectives. (Fancy et al. 2009)

The UCBN consists of nine widely separated NPS units located in western Montana, Idaho, eastern Washington, and central Oregon (Figure 2). The parks in the UCBN include Big Hole National Battlefield (BIHO), City of Rocks National Reserve (CIRO), Craters of the Mon National Monument and Preserve (CRMO), John Day Fossil Beds National Monument (JODA), Hagerman Fossil Beds National Monument (HAFO), Lake Roosevelt National Recreation Area (LARO), Minidoka Internment National Monument (MIIN), Nez Perce National Historical Park (NEPE), and Whitman Mission National Historic Site (WHMI).

The Upper Columbia Basin Network (UCBN) has a large and diverse constituency, including park staff, the scientific community-at-large, and the general public. The UCBN has its own charter which describes the process used to plan, evaluate, and manage the monitoring program. A Board of Directors consisting of park Superintendents, the Regional I&M Coordinator, a member of the Science Advisory Committee, the Deputy Regional Director, and the UCBN Coordinator all oversee the program, its management, and budgetary decisions. The Board acts as an administrative and decision making body, while the Science Advisory Committee (SAC) offers technical assistance and advice to the Board and UCBN parks (Garrett et al. 2007).

Figure 1. UCBN staff demonstrating small mammal trapping techniques to Science Advisory Committee members at an annual meeting at City of Rocks National Reserve.

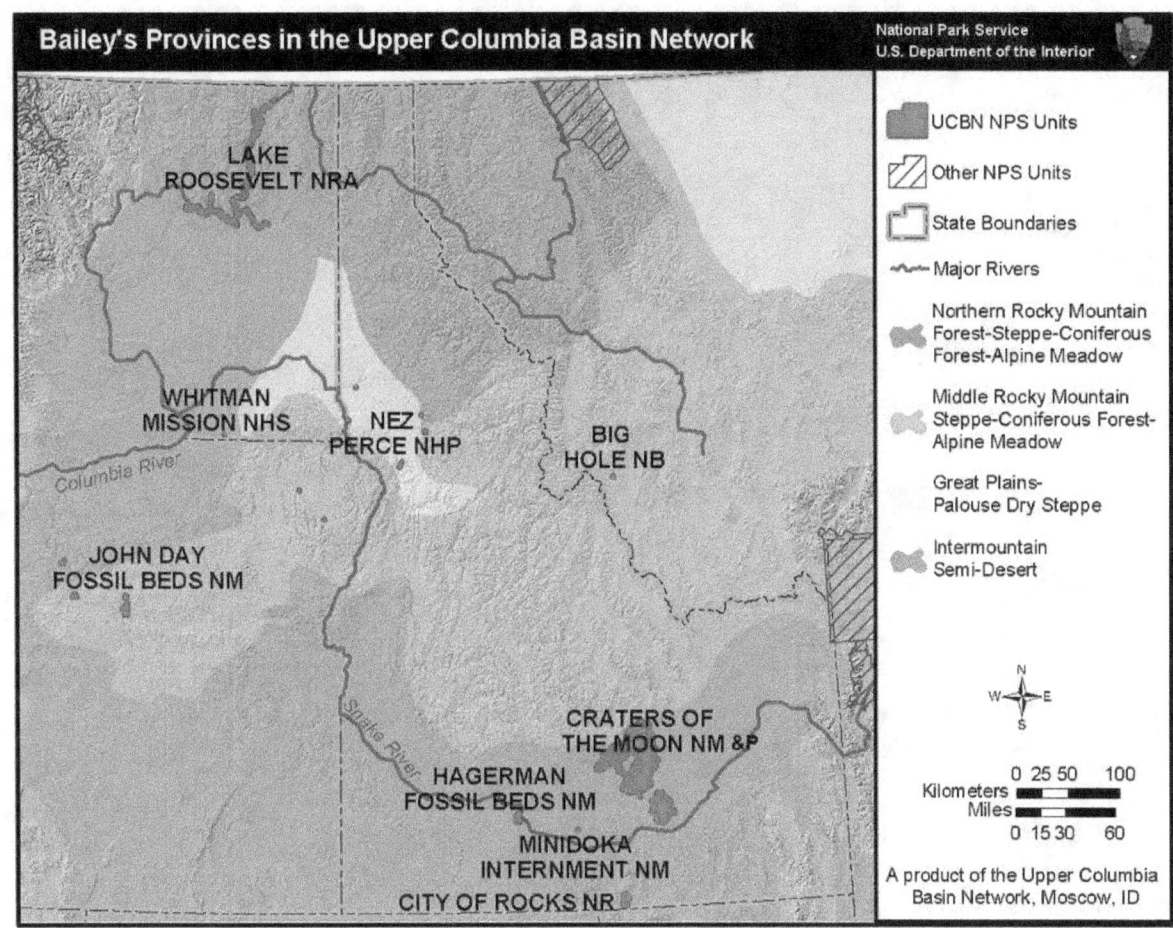

Figure 2. Map of UCBN parks.

UCBN Approach to Science Communication

The UCBN intends to use contemporary, innovative communications strategies to clearly and effectively communicate its discoveries. Scientific data are most meaningful when it is shared with managers, stakeholders, and the public; therefore, only with combined collaborative efforts will the I&M goals and objectives be achieved. Scientific findings must be analyzed, synthesized, and presented in a format which can be easily understood by all interested parties. "Once this information is in our hands, we must share it widely, so that child and adult, amateur and professional can benefit from the knowledge uncovered in these places. The information contained in the parks should help in the surrounding communities, both regional and global, in making choices about their future. Parks and protected places should become increasingly "useful" to surrounding communities as benchmarks and repositories of environmental information" (NPS 1999).

The Upper Columbia Basin Network has adopted an over-arching statement of purpose for its network inventory and monitoring program. This same statement of purpose forms the foundation for its communication strategy.

**Purpose of the Upper Columbia Basin Network
Inventory and Monitoring Program**

The purpose of the UCBN I&M program is to collaboratively develop and conduct scientifically credible inventories and long-term monitoring of park "vital signs" and to distribute this information for use by park staff, partners, and the public, enhancing understanding which leads to sound decision making in the preservation of natural resources and cultural history held in trust by the NPS.

This statement of purpose helps define what the UCBN monitoring program is designed to accomplish, who we are to serve, and where we plan to go from here.

Goals

The intent of this communication plan is primarily to raise awareness and inform internal and external audiences of the UCBN's scientific findings. The following communication goals have been developed specifically to guide the UCBN staff and focus attention on desired programmatic outcomes:

- Generate and disseminate information that advances the management and understanding of natural resources in UCBN parks.
- Identify and conceptualize messages, products, and strategies to facilitate communication between park superintendents and staff, the scientific community, and the general public.
- Raise awareness and promote both the I&M program and the UCBN through emphasizing the importance of natural resource inventory and monitoring.
- Collaborate with park staff to increase efficacy of the content and delivery of UCBN science communications messages.

UCBN Communication Strategy

The large collection of credible scientific data that the UCBN produces each year must be simplified into a concise, clear format for public consumption. The results must be applicable to park managers and decision makers and/or relevant or interesting to non-scientists.

The Information Pyramid

The Information Pyramid helps to illustrate the importance of delivering results appropriate for the selected audience. If the UCBN is to succeed in delivering scientific information to a wide variety of audiences, the communication staff must adhere to the Information Pyramid strategy in carefully choosing when to aggregate scientific information so that policy makers at the top of the pyramid will understand and appreciate the message.

Figure 3 illustrates the process of generating science-based messages to the public. Moving from the bottom to the top of the "pyramid," messages must become simple, clear, and easily understood. The audience changes from the bottom to the top of the "pyramid" from being primarily a scientific audience to the general public, policy makers, and non-scientists.

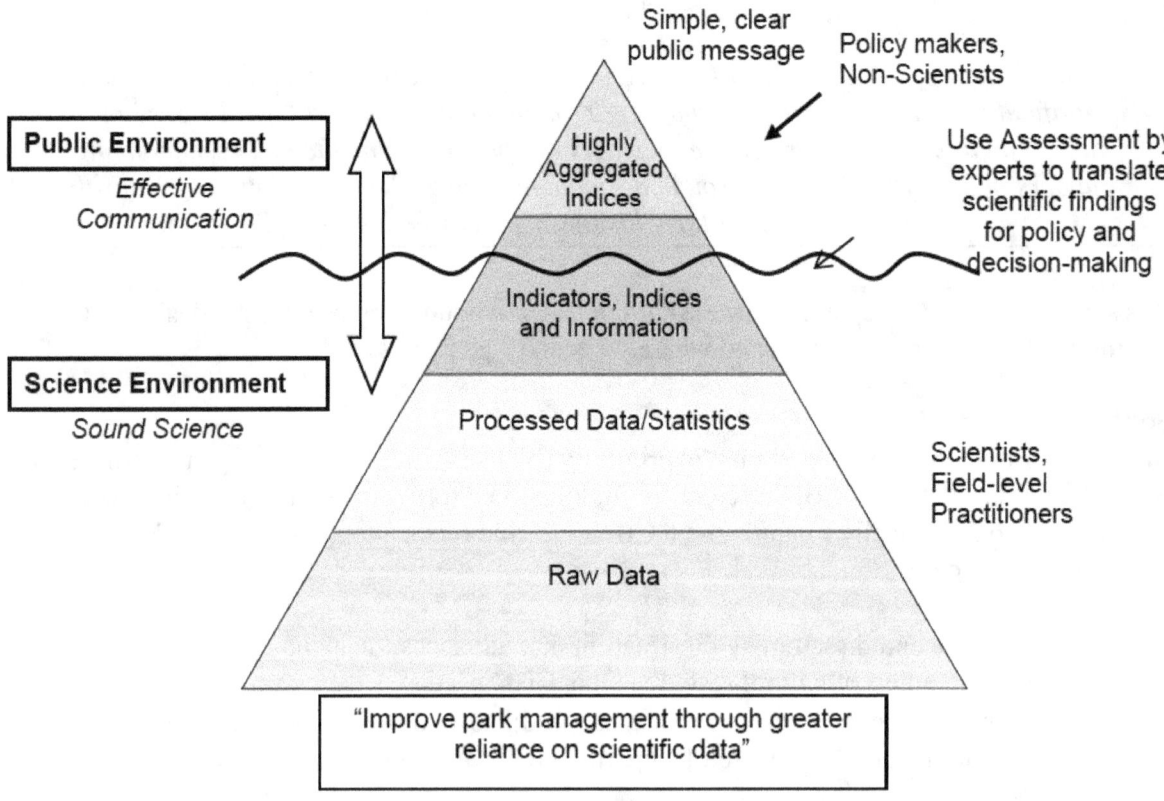

Figure 3. The Information Pyramid (Adapted from Fancy et al. 2009).

The NPS Interpretive Equation

The interpretive equation was developed by the NPS to assist park interpreters (or "rangers" who work directly with the public) in developing interpretive opportunities. The equation is useful for the UCBN to follow in situations where the UCBN will be interacting with the public. The equation is as follows:

$$(Kr + Ka) \times AT = IO$$

Where,

Kr = Knowledge of the resource
Ka = Knowledge of the audience
AT = Appropriate technique
IO = Interpretive Opportunities

The equation states that knowledge of the resource (Kr) combined with knowledge of the audience (Ka) in addition to application of an appropriate technique (AT), leads to interpretive opportunities (IO). This idea will serve as a guide for the development of UCBN products for the public (NPS 2008).

Appropriate Audiences

The primary audiences for UCBN informational material are generally internal audiences (NPS employees) such as park superintendents, resource managers, park interpreters, maintenance staff, law enforcement rangers, and seasonal employees that are involved in the day-to-day operations of a park site. Internal audiences will ultimately judge the success of the UCBN I&M program by whether the scientific information produced is deemed useful to them. For that reason, we contacted our internal audiences early on in the development of this plan to receive their input.

External audiences are those outside the National Park Service and are generally considered a secondary audience. They may include other state and federal partners, park visitors, and local landowners. Effective communication between the UCBN and external audiences will cultivate a sense of stewardship for parks and protected areas in the general public and may provide crucial information relevant to the regional landscape. Secondary audiences are no less important than the primary audience, but with limited resources of time and money, the UCBN must prioritize its communication efforts. Table 2 describes which audiences are internal and which are external.

Table 2. Prioritized grouping of internal and external audiences.

	Internal	External
Primary Audiences		
Superintendents	✕	
Resource managers	✕	
Park interpreters/historians	✕	
Maintenance/facility staff	✕	
Law enforcement rangers	✕	
Other NPS I&M networks	✕	
Seasonal employees	✕	
Secondary Audiences		
Researchers		✕
Educators		✕
Media		✕
Local residents		✕
Park visitors		✕
Special interest groups		✕
Political representatives		✕

NPS Staff Surveys

In 2007, the UCBN contacted interpretive staff at each UCBN park in order to obtain information about the kinds of communication methods, media, and subject matters deemed most useful and desired for specific parks. The product from that first questionnaire was a preliminary needs assessment report which generated ideas about 1) the preferred methods for offering interpretive and educational programs for the public about the monitoring program; 2) which media were considered most appropriate or preferred by parks for disseminating information and messages; and 3) what topics are preferred from a visitors' perspective (Novey 2007). In response to the first question, most UCBN parks indicated flexibility in how monitoring information and results are incorporated into their communications. Six out of nine respondents indicated that a combination of UCBN developed-products, park developed products, and pre-existing products would be acceptable.

Website content was considered the most appropriate media and communication format for UCBN information. Offering website content about the vital signs being specifically monitored at each UCBN park was universally agreed upon as the most appropriate and desired format for sharing UCBN related information. Products oriented toward youth, short written digests of findings intended for the education of park staffs, short/high quality videos, and interactive exhibits were also frequently selected in the top five choices of parks.

Almost all questionnaire respondents placed "the vital signs being monitored at your site" in their top five lists for what they believed would be the most interesting and/or relevant UCBN related topics for visitors to their parks. "Plants (native and exotic) that are being inventoried and/or monitored at your site" was also commonly listed among responses in top five lists for the third question. "Why inventory and monitoring is important, ecosystems, climate change/global warming, animals, and information about how visitors might participate as citizen scientists" were also frequently selected topics.

In addition to the 2007 survey of interpretive staff, an email survey was sent to all UCBN park staff in January 2009 to gain a better understanding of park staff roles, familiarity with the I&M program, and areas of improvement related to UCBN communication. The following questions were asked in the survey:

1. Tell me what you think is unique about your park, and what is your role?
2. Who visits your park? What are these people like, i.e., why do they come, what questions do they ask/information are they seeking?
3. What do you know about the Upper Columbia Basin Network (UCBN) Inventory and Monitoring Program? Have you received information about the UCBN and how?
4. Do you see any benefits of the I&M Program to your work? How could the findings of the I&M Program be helpful/relevant to your work?
5. How would you promote I&M's story to other staff members and visitors?

Twenty-one staff responded out of 140 email recipients (15%). Respondents included chiefs of interpretation, natural and cultural resource managers, law enforcement and education specialists, a unit specialist, administrative staff, superintendents, and park interpreters. Most of the individuals who replied had some contact with the UCBN. Their answers to questions 3, 4, and 5, therefore, were more comprehensive and specific. Overall, responses were positive and helpful.

Some of the most interesting results from the survey were that staff who were familiar with the I&M Program and the UCBN learned about it primarily from the UCBN website and the newsletter. Other sources included: direct contact with UCBN staff and the Board of Directors, direct involvement with current projects, management team meetings, through Science Advisory Committee (SAC) meetings, emails, conversations, a direct link to the UCBN website from an individual park website, informational posters, fieldwork, and park contacts. Several people explained that, unless I&M information directly affects their work, they are generally not up-to-date or interested in sifting through dense scientific information.

The NPS staff survey asked respondents what types of visitors came to their parks and why (Table 3). According to survey responders, the majority of UCBN park visitors do not visit with the intention of learning about natural resources. While most of the UCBN parks were established to protect cultural and paleontological resources, all of the parks have been identified as having significant natural resources, and most have some level of natural resource protection language included in their enabling legislation or other guidance documents.

Table 3. Types of visitors to UCBN parks and reasons for visitation.

Park	Who Visits?	Why? What are they interested in knowing?
BIHO	Westerners (primarily from the Pacific Northwest)	To learn about the battle, personal experience with site, to find closure, US history, American heritage
CIRO	Rock Climbers, recreationalists, hikers historians, drive-by tourists, campers, middle to upper-middle class, Caucasian, 18-55 yrs, school groups, non-profit orgs	Information/location on climbs, recreational opportunities, nature appreciation, CA trail history, ranching, natural history, geology
CRMO	Families, retirees, K-12 students, people driving to/from Yellowstone, 1st time visitors, westerners, extended vacationers	Field trips, geology, flora and fauna, volcanic landscape and history, logistical info., spend 1 day or less
HAFO	Young students, retirees, Idahoans, visiting scientists, researchers, educators	To dig fossils, fossil information, to see fossils, to learn what land was like millions of years ago
JODA	About 50 scientists per year "formally" visit to look at collections, westerners	Research, fossil information
LARO	Regional visitors, school groups, some locals from >100 miles, vacationers, people in campers with laptops, generators, TVs, etc.	Wildlife, learn about noxious weed control, camping/hiking information, beaches, warm temperatures, fishing, recreational boating, history, culture, geology, science, water quality, logistical info.
MIIN	Former internees and their families, westerners	Interested in American internment, to re-visit history, to find closure, personal experience, curiosity, cultural landscape, where is the site? What is there to see?
NEPE	1/2 local, 1/2 non-local, north-westerners, drive-by tourists, tribal members, students, foreign visitors, authors, =/- 20,000/year	Nez Perce history, Chief Joseph, cultural artifacts, history, stories, to find closure, Lewis and Clark expedition, locals bringing non-locals, Nez Perce war, 1803-06 exploration, what else is there to see/do in the area?
WHMI	School groups, 55,000/year, family groups, tribal members	Martyrdom information, natural resources, history, texts/references, American settlement in E. OR, quiet walks, educational experiences, Whitmans, Oregon Trail, Cayuse people

UCBN Science Communication Methods

The following communication products have been developed and are in use by the UCBN as of May 2009 (Table 4). Below each listed product we include 1) key topics, messages, and themes that each convey; 2) guidelines for production and distribution of each product or service; 3) principal author(s), and 4) primary audience and review process. All of these products are designed to raise awareness of the services of the UCBN I & M program and inspire interest among park staff and stakeholders. The UCBN staff strives to demonstrate their hard work, passion, and professionalism in each report produced for the parks. Finally, the products described below seek to cultivate a sense of stewardship of park resources, assist in place-based education, and promote public engagement.

A. Annual Administrative Report and Work Plan (AARWP)

Key topics, messages, and themes to be conveyed:

Figure 4. UCBN and park staff at JODA discuss upcoming plans.

- Budgets help guide protocol development, fieldwork initiatives, communication, and all UCBN programs.
- Coordination and communication between and among groups results in program efficiency and monetary savings.
- Parks, UCBN, and regional staff should communicate their needs and goals with each other.

Guidelines for the production and distribution of the Annual Administrative Report and Work Plan (AARWP):
- Produced annually at the end of the fiscal year in September.
- Format of the AARWP is determined by servicewide I&M program managers.
- Copies of the AARWP are distributed to superintendents, SAC members, UCBN staff, the regional coordinator, and servicewide I&M program managers.

Principal author(s):
- This report is written by the UCBN Coordinator with help from other staff members (where applicable).

Primary audience and review process:
- Internal audience, reviewed and approved by PWR I&M Coordinator, WASO Program Manager, and UCBN Board of Directors.

B. Monitoring Protocol Narrative and SOPs

Key topics, messages, and themes:

- Contain specific analytical tools for interpreting and presenting monitoring data.
- Address assumptions regarding the target population and the level of confidence desired or sampling variability. These criteria are described more fully in the UCBN's Vital Signs Monitoring Plan (Garrett et al. 2007).
- Include step-by-step standard operating procedures (SOPs) and narratives which describe more fully the significance of the inventory and monitoring effort and the methods required to implement the protocol.
- Focus on a single vital sign.

Guidelines for the production and distribution of protocol narratives and SOPs:

- Frequency of production is based on protocol development schedule (Garrett et. al. 2007).
- All protocols follow the NPS Natural Resource Publications Natural Resource Report (NRR) template.
- Protocols and SOPs should be well-written and easy to follow for field technicians and resource managers.
- Hard copies of protocols and SOPs are distributed to park managers (at parks where monitoring occurs) and at least two copies are kept at the UCBN office.
- Final protocols and SOPs are posted on the UCBN website and distributed electronically to all stakeholders.
- A customized Microsoft Access relational database application is developed for each protocol and is designed to store and manipulate the data associated with each protocol.
- All project data are certified for accuracy and completeness prior to development of final reports.
- All GIS mapping products follow the NPS template for producing maps with ESRI ArcGIS or ArcView software available at http://imgis.nps.gov/templates.html.
- All protocols and SOPs are peer-reviewed and posted to the NatureBib website when finalized.

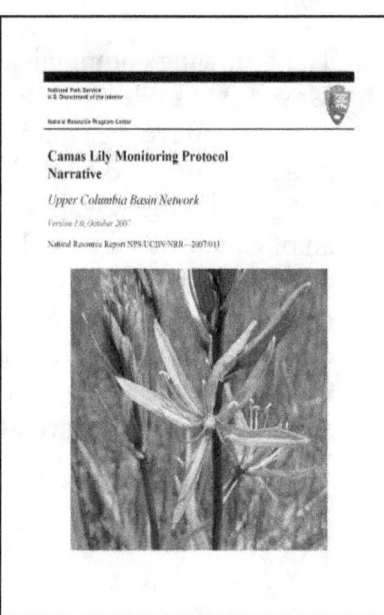

Figure 5. Camas lily monitoring protocol narrative.

Principal author(s):

- Protocols are written by UCBN staff, contractors, and cooperators.

Primary audience and review process:

- Internal audience, peer reviewed internally by UCBN and park staff, submitted to the regional coordinator for external peer review before final approval for implementation is granted.

C. Monitoring Annual Reports

Key topics, messages, and themes:

- Document the collection, analyses, and interpretation of monitoring data.
- Document annual monitoring effort and activities, including any changes to the protocols, and describe the current status of monitoring results (Garrett et al. 2007).
- Intended for greater, in-depth understanding of vital sign monitoring.
- Annual data compilation for each protocol.
- Provide annual distribution maps and other measured attributes.
- Evaluate data quality and identify any data quality concerns and/or deviations from protocols that affect data quality and interpretability.

Figure 6. 2008 camas monitoring annual report.

Guidelines for the production and distribution of monitoring annual reports:

- Monitoring reports are produced annually for any protocol where data collection has occurred.
- All monitoring reports follow the NPS Natural Resource Publications Natural Resource Technical Report (NRTR) template.
- Monitoring reports should be well-written and easy to understand for UCBN and park staff.
- Hard copies of monitoring reports are distributed to park managers (at parks where monitoring occurs).
- Monitoring reports are posted on the UCBN website and distributed electronically to park staff.
- All project data are certified for accuracy and completeness prior to development of annual reports.
- All GIS mapping products follow the NPS template for producing maps with ESRI ArcGIS or ArcView software is available at http://imgis.nps.gov/templates.html.
- Information is provided to parks in time for park Government Performance Results Act (GPRA) goals reporting and for informing and evaluating park resource stewardship strategies.
- All monitoring reports are peer reviewed and posted to the NatureBib website when finalized.

Principal author(s):

- Annual reports are written by UCBN staff, contractors, and cooperators.

Primary audience and review process:

- All audiences (internal and external), peer reviewed internally by UCBN and park staff before being submitted for regional level review by a key official.

D. Monitoring Trend Analysis and Synthesis Reports

Key topics, messages, and themes:
- In depth status and trend analysis.
- Evaluate findings in relationship to park long-term management and restoration goals.
- Evaluate operational aspects of the monitoring program.

Guidelines for the production and distribution of monitoring trend analysis and synthesis reports:
- Produced approximately every three-five years or as the importance of emerging information warrants.
- All trend reports follow the NPS Natural Resource Publications Natural Resource Technical Report (NRTR) template.
- Hard copies of protocols and SOPs are distributed to park managers (at parks where monitoring occurs) and at least two copies are kept at the UCBN office.
- Final reports are posted on the UCBN website and distributed electronically to all stakeholders.
- All project data are certified for accuracy and completeness prior to development of analysis and synthesis reports.
- All GIS mapping products follow the NPS template for producing maps with ESRI ArcGIS or ArcView software available at http://imgis.nps.gov/templates.html.
- All trend reports are peer-reviewed and posted to the NatureBib website when finalized.

Principal author(s):
- Trend reports are written by UCBN staff, contractors, and cooperators.

Primary audience and review process:
- All audiences (internal and external), peer reviewed internally by UCBN and park staff before being submitted for regional level review by a key official.

E. Resource Briefs

Key topics, messages, and themes:
- Explore protocol-specific topics.
- Describe how monitoring data informs resource management.
- Provide data summary and analysis tables.

Guidelines for the production and distribution of resource briefs:
- Format for briefs follow the UCBN template (sections, fonts, graphics, etc.).
- Resource briefs include the following sections:
  - UCBN parks where resource is being monitored
  - The importance of vital sign/monitoring efforts
  - Status and trends
  - Monitoring objectives
  - Management applications
  - Contact information
- Resource briefs are prepared promptly at the end of each field season.
- Resource briefs are distributed to all interested stakeholders via email, mail, and hand delivery and are posted to the UCBN website.
- Resource briefs are distributed at conferences, workshops, symposia, alongside informational posters, and at parks for staff and the public.
- Resource briefs serve as the most widely circulated UCBN communication product. As such, they must be professional and written clearly for a non-technical audience.
- Resource briefs are distributed annually at the UCBN Science Day in October.
- Resource briefs are provided to park interpretive staff for distribution to interested visitors.
- All project data are certified for accuracy and completeness prior to development of resource briefs.
- All briefs are printed on semi-gloss paper for a professional, finished appearance.

Principal author(s):
- Resource briefs are written by UCBN staff, contractors, and cooperators.

Primary audience and review process:
- All audiences (internal and external), peer reviewed internally by UCBN and park staff.

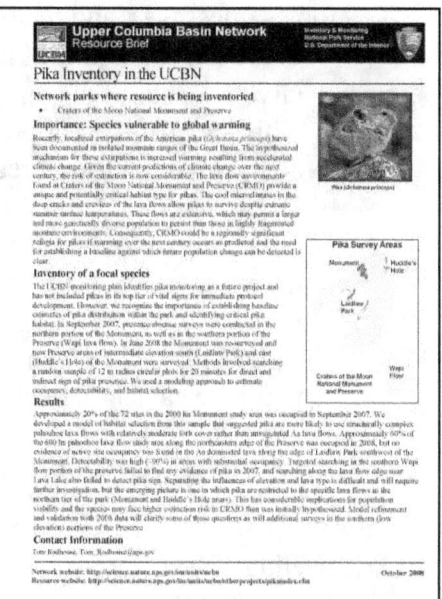

Figure 7. Pika inventory resource brief.

F. Annual Science Day

Key topics, messages, and themes:
- Share annual results of monitoring.
- Give park staff the opportunity to interact with scientists developing protocols and/or analyzing monitoring results.
- Discuss current natural resource issues.
- Educate park staff and stakeholders about the value of natural resource inventory and monitoring.
- Build bridges between individual parks and facilitate camaraderie amongst UCBN and park staff.

Figure 8. UCBN Board of Directors and Science Advisory Committee at the 2008 Science Day held in Moscow, Idaho.

Guidelines for the production of the annual science day meeting:
- The UCBN annual science day is held in October each year. The meeting location is set by the UCBN board of directors with input from the Science Advisory Committee (SAC).
- All UCBN board members and park staff are invited and encouraged to attend.
- All annual reports and powerpoint presentations are distributed to key stakeholders during the first day of the meeting and are posted on the UCBN website immediately following the meeting.
- Park managers are encouraged to present annual updates on park resources and projects.
- Paper copies of the UCBN newsletter and resource briefs are available to all attendees.
- Nametags are provided for each participant.
- A slideshow of photos of UCBN staff, collaborators, and monitoring efforts is produced each year for the meeting (UCBN Year In Review).

Principal organizer(s):
- UCBN staff.

Primary audience and review process:
- All audiences (internal and external), attended by UCBN staff, SAC members, and the UCBN Board of Directors.

20

G. Internet Website

Key topics, messages, and themes:
- Promote communication, coordination, and collaboration among UCBN staff, park staff, and the public.
- Educate park staff and stakeholders about the value of natural resource inventory and monitoring efforts.
- Provide a valuable resource for the scientific community to obtain monitoring information in a timely manner.

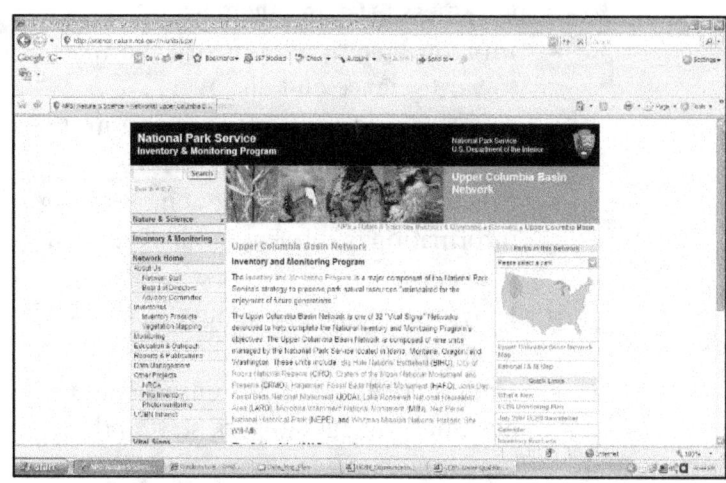

Figure 9. UCBN internet homepage.

Guidelines for the production and distribution of website information:
- Only data subjected to full quality control are posted.
- Sensitive data are protected from unauthorized access.
- Contact information is readily available and easy to find.
- New information is posted as soon as it is available.
- UCBN data manager reviews the website quarterly for accuracy, additions, and uploading new information.
- Dreamweaver is the main computer program used to update the website. The UCBN template is followed to make updating information easy and convenient.
- The website serves as a centralized repository for all finalized reports and summaries which do not contain sensitive information (Garrett et al. 2007).
- The website is periodically evaluated by park staff to determine the interpretability, usefulness, and relevance of the data presented.
- The website follows NPS I&M webpage formatting standards.

Principal organizer(s):
- UCBN data manager.

Primary audience and review process:
- All audiences (internal and external), peer reviewed internally by UCBN and park staff.

H. Newsletter

Key topics, messages, and themes:

- Promote a spirit of curiosity and wonder toward science and discovery.
- Emphasize the importance of natural resource inventory and monitoring efforts.
- Educate readers about how monitoring information is informing management decisions.
- Provide information about the status of UCBN monitoring projects.
- Communicate UCBN's purpose and accomplishments to park staff and the public.

Guidelines for the production and distribution of the newsletter:

- Distributed biannually (January and July) via email and posted to the UCBN website.

- Approximately 75-100 hard copies are provided to individual parks, as well as distributed at meetings.

Figure 10. July 2008 *Basin Bulletin*, the UCBN's biannual newsletter.

- Follows the UCBN template (graphics, fonts, length, etc.) in Adobe InDesign.
- Format and content are evaluated periodically with park staff to determine the interpretability, usefulness, and relevance of the information presented.
- Park staff and researchers are invited to contribute articles for the newsletter.
- Newsletters should be attractive and casual, yet informative and science-based.
- An example newsletter is included in Appendix B.

Principal organizer(s):

- UCBN science communication specialist.

Primary audience and review process:

- All audiences (internal and external), peer reviewed internally by UCBN staff.

I. Scientific Publications and Presentations

Key topics, messages, and themes:

- Communicate advances in knowledge.
- Present innovative monitoring techniques.
- Describe the importance of natural resource inventory and monitoring and how results are informing management decisions.
- Provide information on the status of UCBN projects.
- Establish connections, similarities, and differences between the natural resources of UCBN parks and why a network monitoring approach is most appropriate.

Figure 11. Vital signs scoping workshop held at the University of Idaho in 2006.

Guidelines for the production and distribution of scientific publications and presentations:

- The UCBN staff will present and publish the scientific results of their monitoring efforts at conferences and in peer reviewed journal publications, whenever feasible.
- All presentations, posters, and publications are made available on the UCBN website as soon as they have been displayed, submitted, and/or presented as permitted by copyright restrictions.
- All scientific publications are peer reviewed either by UCBN staff or external peer reviewers for accuracy and quality.
- All publications should display the UCBN and NPS arrowhead logo, and include the UCBN website address.
- All publications and presentations are sent via email and/or mail to park superintendents and resource managers when monitoring efforts affect their parks.
- All project data are certified for accuracy and completeness.

Principal author(s)/organizer(s):

- UCBN staff.

Primary audience and review process:

- All audiences (internal and external), peer reviewed internally by UCBN staff.

J. Informational Posters

Key topics, messages, and themes:
- Promote a spirit of curiosity and wonder toward science and discovery.
- Emphasize the importance of natural resource inventory and monitoring efforts.
- Educate readers about how monitoring information is informing management decisions.
- Provide information about the status of UCBN monitoring projects.
- Communicate UCBN's purpose and accomplishments to park staff and the public.

Figure 12. Sagebrush-steppe field monitoring informational poster.

Guidelines for the production and distribution of informational posters:
- Informational posters are provided for each protocol being monitored.
- Posters follow the UCBN template (graphics, fonts, content, etc.).
- Posters are available on the UCBN website.
- Poster content and format are periodically evaluated with park staff to determine the interpretability, usefulness, and relevance of the information presented.
- Posters are displayed in park Visitor Centers.
- Resource briefs are provided as a handout alongside the poster for interested readers to take home with them.
- UCBN staff will ensure that park staff are briefed on information presented on posters—this is done via a short informational session with staff when UCBN staff deliver the poster to the park.
- Posters are printed at the UCBN office on the plotter printer.
- See Appendix D for example informational poster.

Principal author(s):
- UCBN staff.

Primary audience and review process:
- All audiences (internal and external), peer reviewed internally by UCBN and park staff.

K. Brochures

Key topics, messages, and themes:
- Provide information about the importance of collecting natural resource inventory and monitoring data to inform management decisions.
- Provide information about the status of UCBN projects.
- Communicate UCBN's purpose and accomplishments to park staff and the public.

Figure 13. UCBN brochure.

Guidelines for the production and distribution of brochures:
- The first UCBN brochure was created in 2006. An annual review is conducted to determine if this brochure needs updated.
- Brochure is available on the UCBN website.
- Brochure content and format is periodically evaluated with park staff to determine the interpretability, usefulness, and relevance of the information presented.
- Brochure is distributed to parks for interested visitors and staff.
- Brochure is printed on semi-gloss or glossy paper for a professional, finished look.

Principal author(s):
- UCBN staff.

Primary audience and review process:
- All audiences (internal and external), peer reviewed internally by UCBN and park staff.

L. News Articles/Press Releases

Key topics, messages, and themes:

- Promote a spirit of curiosity and wonder toward science and discovery.
- Emphasize the importance of natural resource inventory and monitoring efforts.
- Educate readers about how monitoring information is informing management decisions.
- Provide information about the status of UCBN monitoring projects.
- Communicate UCBN's purpose and accomplishments to park staff and the public.

Figure 14. LARO 2007 park newspaper.

Guidelines for the production and distribution of news articles/press releases:

- Always include reference to the National Park Service, the I&M program, and the Upper Columbia Basin Network.
- Ensure that park staffs are aware of all scientific publications, presentations, news articles, or press releases that mention park resources.
- All articles are available on the UCBN website and circulated to park superintendents and staff.
- Content of all articles and press releases must be approved by park superintendents before being released to the general public.
- A display of all articles and press releases involving UCBN staff during the last year is presented at the annual science day meeting in October.

Principal author(s):

- UCBN staff.

Primary audience and review process:

- All audiences (internal and external), peer reviewed internally by UCBN and park superintendents.

M. Products with UCBN Logo

Key topics, messages, and themes:
- Promote UCBN logo recognition by citizen scientist students, volunteers, resource managers, superintendents, park staff, and cooperators/stakeholders.
- Provide thank you/appreciation gift for volunteers.

Guidelines for production and distribution of logo products:
- Each product will display logo with UCBN name, acronym, and easily-recognizable icon/picture.
- All scientific publications, presentations, CDS, multimedia, important letters or emails, and posters will display the UCBN and/or the NPS arrowhead logo.
- Outdoor products will be sturdy and conspicuous.
- Office-related products will look professional.
- Citizen scientists will receive a token of appreciation that displays the UCBN logo.
- Items will be functional and fairly inexpensive.

Figure 15. Coffee mug imprinted with the UCBN logo.

Principal developer(s):
- UCBN staff.

Primary audience and review process:
- All audiences (internal and external), reviewed for cost and purpose by UCBN staff.

N. Park Site Visits/Brown Bag Lunches

Key topics, messages, and themes:
- Provide information about the importance of collecting natural resource inventory and monitoring data to inform management decisions.
- Provide information about the status of UCBN projects.
- Communicate UCBN's purpose and accomplishments to park staff.
- Offer park staff the opportunity to ask questions, discuss natural resource related issues with UCBN staff, and provide recommendations for future communications strategies.
- Help park staff learn about and communicate the purpose and results of monitoring to the public.
- Create and maintain a favorable sentiment that the UCBN provides an important service to each of the UCBN parks.

Guidelines for park site visits and brown bag lunches:
- Periodic annual park site visits/brown bag lunches are scheduled for the purpose of meeting with available park staff to discuss the monitoring program. A face-to-face meeting enables UCBN staff to communicate the purpose and results of the UCBN monitoring program.

- All monitoring crews will try to attend a park interpretive program at the beginning of their field work in each park so that they are familiar with the park and its resources, as described to park visitors.
- UCBN field crews will request a welcome orientation for staff to meet monitoring crews.
- UCBN field crews will incorporate discussions of the monitoring program into conversations with park staff.
- UCBN field crews will wear clothing that clearly identifies them as UCBN and/or NPS employees.
- UCBN field crews will distribute literature, including brochures, newsletters, resource briefs, posters, and/or reports at parks for interested staff and visitors.
- When feasible, UCBN field crews will invite park staff to watch or be involved with monitoring activities.
- All monitoring crews will carry a NPS scientific research and collection permit when conducting monitoring activities at a park site.

Principal developer(s):
- UCBN staff.

Primary audience and review process:
- All audiences (internal and external), peer reviewed internally by UCBN staff.

O. Email and Telephone Correspondence

Key topics, messages, and themes:
- Correspond with internal and external audiences in a timely manner.
- Inform park staff about field work schedules and data collection efforts.
- Communicate the latest findings to peers.
- Identify emerging issues and generate new ideas.

Figure 16. Email correspondence is one of the fastest and easiest communication techniques.

Guidelines for production and distribution of emails:
- Response to all emails will occur in a timely manner.
- Professional language will be used at all times.
- Attachments will be virus-free and office-appropriate.
- Emails will be sent regularly (daily, weekly, monthly) to update superintendents and park staff on new I&M information, regulations, findings, etc.
- Appropriate park staff will be notified of upcoming park site visits.
- Contact information will be provided at the bottom of each email.
- UCBN letterhead will be used when appropriate.

Principal developer(s):
- UCBN staff.

Primary audience and review process:
- All audiences (internal and external), peer reviewed internally by UCBN staff when appropriate.

P. Citizen Science Programs
Key topics, messages, and themes:
- For Citizen Scientists:
  -Gain hands-on experience in scientific research.
  -Use technology to gather, display and analyze data (GPS, compass, etc.).
  -Contribute positively to the environment.
  -Work with natural resource professionals and expose citizens to careers in the sciences.
  -Have fun participating in a service learning project.

Figure 17. Citizen Scientists and NPS staff monitoring camas at Weippe Prairie (NEPE).

  -Cultivate a sense of park stewardship
- For the Parks:
  -Develop a sustainable, long term monitoring project.
  -Take a holistic approach to managing park resources, viewing them as both culturally and naturally significant.
  -Restore or maintain a natural resource for future generations.
  -Develop an informed and concerned local citizen volunteer base.
- Promote a spirit of curiosity and wonder toward science and discovery.
- Emphasize the importance of natural resource inventory and monitoring efforts.
- Provide information about the status of UCBN monitoring projects.
- Communicate UCBN's purpose and accomplishments.
- An effort should be made to expose all citizen science field teams to a park interpretive program so that they are familiar with the park and its resources, as described to park visitors.
- Relate all curriculum lessons/work to academic standards criteria.

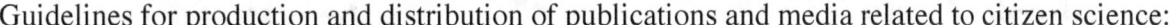

Guidelines for production and distribution of publications and media related to citizen science:
- Teachers, parents, students, and collaborators will be consulted about the content of citizen science programs.
- Local communities will be notified about UCBN-related events through local news sources (i.e., radio, television, paper, magazines, etc.) when appropriate.
- Environmental education agencies will be approached about collaborative opportunities to provide citizen science programs.
- When feasible, UCBN staff will assist teachers with development of lesson plans related to citizen science programs and field work (e.g., Camas Citizen Science Monitoring Program high school level lesson plans).

- Annual funding from the NPS Volunteers-In-Parks (VIP) Program will be used to strengthen the UCBN citizen science program. "The primary purpose of the VIP program is to provide a vehicle through which the National Park Service can accept and utilize voluntary help and services from the public. The major objective of the program is to utilize this voluntary help in such a way that is mutually beneficial to the National Park Service and the volunteer" (NPS 2009b). The UCBN will promote, acknowledge, and utilize this important program, whenever possible.
- A photo release form will be provided for all students under the age of 18 so that photos can be published or used beyond the scope of internal reports created by the UCBN.
- The UCBN will jointly report year-end VIP funding results with NEPE.

Principal Developer(s):
- UCBN staff.

Primary Audience and Review Process:
- All audiences (internal and external), peer reviewed internally by UCBN and park staff.

Q. Image Database

Key topics, messages, and themes:
- UCBN parks are unique.
- UCBN staff visit and collect data across nine parks in a variety of landscape types and ecosystems.
- Promote a spirit of curiosity and wonder toward science and discovery.
- Show professionalism.
- Illustrate how the UCBN uses current technologies for data collection and analysis.
- UCBN parks have distinct histories and resources.
- Contributions of park staff, citizen scientists, volunteers, UCBN staff, and other stakeholders to the NPS I&M program.
- Education, interpretation, and communication are all important to the UCBN.

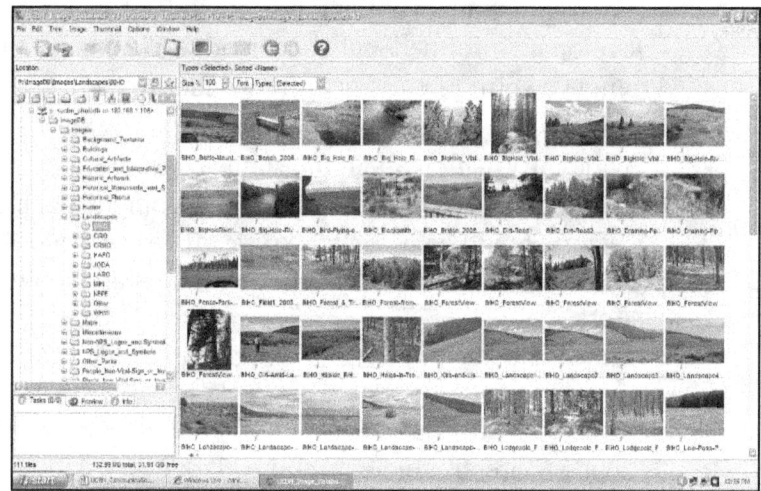

Figure 18. Screenshot of the UCBN's ThumbsPlus photo database.

Guidelines for using the photo database:
- Photos are uploaded to the ThumbsPlus 7 software program, which facilitates searching on file names and keywords, and stored in a well-organized directory structure on the UCBN Network Attached Storage (NAS) device.
- Photos are easily discoverable and obtainable.
- Photos not yet subjected to full quality control are not released.
- Sensitive data are identified and protected from unauthorized access.
- Clear guidelines for the ownership and sharing of data and information are established.
- Photos will be organized in folders, based on their content and park association (background textures; buildings; cultural artifacts; education and interpretive programs; etc.) Each photo is associated with a list of keywords as already set up in the ThumbsPlus software program. Each photo may be queried under "user field" information, including: project, subject, park code (4-letter park designation), location, common name, species name, photographer, distribution restrictions, credits, storage location of original, description, etc.). See the ThumbsPlus 7 user manual for further information on database organization (http://www.thumbsplus.com/download.shtml). A user manual is available on the NAS shared storage system at the UCBN office.

Principal Developer(s):
- UCBN science communication specialist and staff.

Primary Audience and Review Process:
- All audiences (internal and external), peer reviewed internally by UCBN staff.

R. Interpretation and Outreach

Key topics, messages, and themes:
- Promote communication, coordination, and collaboration among various NPS program areas related to inventory and monitoring.
- Emphasize the importance of natural resource inventory and monitoring efforts.
- Provide information about the status of UCBN projects.
- Help parks publicly convey new and ongoing scientific research into interpretive programs.
- Education, interpretation, and communication are all important to the UCBN.
- Promote a spirit of curiosity and wonder toward science and discovery.
- Describe how UCBN monitoring results are informing management decisions.

Figure 19. Interpreters can use current UCBN data to inform their audiences about the status and trends of natural resources in their parks.

- Give non-technical audiences an opportunity to appreciate and understand the importance of natural resources.

Guidelines for production and distribution of interpretation and outreach materials:
- UCBN staff will participate in park scoping, meetings, workshops, and festivals, when appropriate.
- Chiefs of Interpretation are invited to attend the annual UCBN Science Days.
- The "Basin Bulletin" and resource briefs are distributed to park interpretive staff.
- Citizen science monitoring programs are promoted with park education specialists, interpreters, and volunteer organizations.
- Relevant papers, posters, and presentations produced or used by UCBN staff are distributed to interested interpretive staff.
- UCBN information disseminated to interpretive staff and the public, is clear, concise, and relevant.
- The UCBN will promote, acknowledge, and utilize park interpretive programs, whenever possible.

Principal organizer/developer(s):
- UCBN science communication specialist and staff.

Primary audience and review process:
- All audiences (internal and external), peer reviewed internally by UCBN and park staff.

Table 4. Summary of UCBN communications methods.

Communication Method	Objectives	Primary Audience	Frequency	Review Process
A. Annual Administrative Report and Work Plan	·Account for funds and FTEs expended ·Describe objectives, tasks, accomplishments, products of the monitoring effort ·Improve communication within park, network, and region	Internal audience	Annual - October	Reviewed and approved by PWR I&M Coordinator, WASO Program Manager, and UCBN Board of Directors
B. Monitoring Protocol Narrative and SOPs	·Direct monitoring operations ·Describe sampling design, field methods, data handling, analysis, and reporting, personnel requirements, training, and operational requirements ·Describe rationale and objectives for monitoring	Internal audience	Commensurate with protocol development schedule	Peer reviewed internally by UCBN and park staff, submitted to the regional coordinator for external peer review before final approval for implementation is granted
C. Monitoring Annual Reports	·Describe and communicate annual monitoring effort ·Document changes in monitoring protocols or provide recommendations for necessary changes ·Determine patterns/trends in resource condition	All audiences (internal and external)	Annual	Peer reviewed internally by UCBN and park staff before submitting for regional level review by a key official.

Table 4. Summary of UCBN communications methods (continued).

Communication Method	Objectives	Primary Audience	Frequency	Review Process
D. Monitoring Trend Analysis and Synthesis Reports	·Synthesis of 5 years of annual data collection efforts to assess trends ·Recommend management actions if needed (feedback for adaptive management)	All audiences (internal and external)	3-5 year intervals for resources sampled annually	Peer reviewed internally by UCBN and park staff before submitting for regional level review by a key official
E. Resource Briefs	·Describe monitoring methods and status of the resource ·One page synopsis of monitoring strategy and results	All audiences (internal and external)	Annual	Peer reviewed internally by UCBN and park staff
F. Annual Science Day	·Review and summarize information on UCBN vital signs ·Identify emerging issues and generate new ideas ·Facilitate interactions among park staff, park superintendents, UCBN staff, contractors, and cooperators	All audiences (internal and external) Science advisory committee members, UCBN staff, park superintendents, park staff, research scientists, contractors, and cooperators	Annual	Attended by UCBN staff, science advisory committee members, and the UCBN Board of Directors

Table 4. Summary of UCBN communications methods (continued).

Communication Method	Objectives	Primary Audience	Frequency	Review Process
G. Internet Website	·Centralized repository for all final reports to ensure products are easily accessible in commonly-used electronic formats ·Provide current information on UCBN activities including newsletters, contact information, schedule for monitoring activities, etc.	All audiences (internal and external) Superintendents, park staff, UCBN staff, servicewide program managers, contractors, cooperators, and general public	Quarterly or as reports are finalized and require posting	Peer reviewed internally by UCBN and park staff
H. Newsletters	·Review and summarize network activities and findings of general interest ·Describe the role and purpose of monitoring natural resources to non-technical audiences	All audiences (internal and external) Park staff, agency partners, cooperators, interpreters, and general public	Biannually (January and July)	Peer reviewed internally by UCBN staff
I. Scientific Publications and Presentations	·Document and communicate advances in knowledge ·Review and summarize information on a specific topic or subject area ·Communicate latest findings to peers	All audiences (internal and external) Science Advisory Committee members, UCBN staff, park superintendents, park staff, research scientists, contractors, and cooperators	Variable	External peer review by journal editor if papers are published, presentations will be internally peer reviewed by UCBN staff

Table 4. Summary of UCBN communications methods (continued).

Communication Method	Objectives	Primary Audience	Frequency	Review Process
J. Informational Posters	·Describe the role and purpose of the I&M Program to non-technical audiences ·Help the public understand how scientific monitoring assists NPS managers in making informed decisions	All audiences (internal and external) Park staff, agency partners, cooperators, and general public	Variable	Peer reviewed internally by UCBN and park staff
K. Brochures	·Describe the role and purpose of the I&M Program to non-technical audiences ·Help the public understand how scientific monitoring assists NPS managers in making informed decisions	All audiences (internal and external) Park staff, agency partners, cooperators, and general public	Variable (updated as needed)	Peer reviewed internally by UCBN and park staff
L. News Articles/Press Releases	·Describe the role and purpose of the I&M Program to non-technical audiences ·Help the public understand how scientific monitoring assists NPS managers in making informed decisions	All audiences (internal and external) Park staff, agency partners, cooperators, and general public	Variable	Peer reviewed internally by UCBN and park superintendents
M. Products with UCBN Logo	·Graphical element designed for immediate recognition for public ·Identify the UCBN as part of the National Park Service	All audiences (internal and external) UCBN staff, park staff, and volunteers	Variable	Reviewed for cost and purpose by UCBN staff

Table 4. Summary of UCBN communications methods (continued).

Communication Method	Objectives	Primary Audience	Frequency	Review Process
N. Park Site Visits/Brown Bag Lunches	·Meet and discuss park resource issues with managers, staff, and visitors	All audiences (internal and external) Park staff, agency partners, cooperators, and general public	Variable, depending on availability of park staff	Peer reviewed internally by UCBN staff
O. Email and Telephone Correspondence	·Reach stakeholders in a timely manner ·Inform park staff about field work schedules and data collection efforts ·Communicate latest findings to peers ·Identify emerging issues and generate new ideas	All audiences (internal and external) Park staff, agency partners, cooperators, and general public	Continual	Peer reviewed internally by UCBN staff when appropriate
P. Citizen Science Programs	·Describe the role and purpose of the I&M Program to non-technical audiences ·Engage volunteers in the long-term scientific monitoring of natural resources in UCBN parks ·Collaborate with park staff, schools, and outreach programs	All audiences (internal and external) Park staff, agency partners, cooperators, citizen volunteers, and general public	Variable, depending on monitoring protocol requirements	Peer reviewed internally by UCBN and park staff

Table 4. Summary of UCBN communications methods (continued).

Communication Method	Objectives	Primary Audience	Frequency	Review Process
Q. Image Database	·Document UCBN accomplishments	All audiences (internal and external)	Variable	Peer reviewed internally by UCBN staff
	·Provide UCBN and park staff with high quality images for reports, promotional information, etc.	Park staff, agency partners, cooperators, and general public		
	·Increase efficiency			
	·Enhance delivery of messages to park staff and the public			
R. Interpretation and Outreach	·Inform the public about monitoring efforts of park natural resources	All audiences (internal and external)	Variable	Peer reviewed internally by UCBN and park staff
	·Integrate science communication efforts between the I&M program and parks	Park staff, agency partners, cooperators, and general public		
	·Improve shared communications messages with parks			

Potential Future UCBN Communication Products and Tools
Many of the following recommendations were offered either through the UCBN email survey or through a preliminary scoping workshop conducted during a UCBN Chief of Interpretation meeting organized by the network's Interpretive Resource Advisory Committee representative in January 2009. These initial scoping sessions included interpreters, education specialists, and other park staff.

- QuickTime movie about general UCBN information (podcasts)
- QuickTime movies about each UCBN vital sign (podcasts)
- E-bulletin (email updates with bulleted I&M highlights)
- Visitor center displays and information
  -Assistance with creating a rotating informational display at JODA and NEPE
  -Collaboration with CRMO for natural resource management museum exhibit
- Conduct annual question/answer sessions with parks and I&M staff
  -Interpretation-focused training
  -Special UCBN programs at parks for general audiences
- All presentations and posters posted on UCBN website
- Provide kids' content via the website such as the "Featured Creature"
- Digital picture archive of park inventory and monitoring posted on UCBN website
- Virtual learning center
- UCBN exhibits at park festivals and fairs
- Waysides
- Environmental education programs for classrooms
- Work with interpreters to accomplish goals related to the NPS Centennial Initiative

UCBN Image Database

The UCBN image database contains photos of current monitoring projects, line drawings depicting vital signs, logos used in informational literature, and other graphics that might be of use when creating communication products. The database operates using the software ThumbsPlus Pro 7. This database aids UCBN staff in cataloging images that will be of value to the UCBN or that will fill gaps in the dissemination of information about UCBN activities. By U.S. law, all UCBN owned images are in the public domain. Access to the image database is currently limited to UCBN staff for logistical and data security reasons. All inquiries concerning the use of the database should be referred to a UCBN staff member.

One of the keys to the success of the image database is to have the UCBN science communications specialist regularly curate the database to add new images and delete old, inferior images, and to identify gaps where the UCBN could use more images of a certain subject matter. As with any collection, quality is considered more important over quantity. A user guide was developed for the image database and is available from the UCBN science communication specialist (Novey and Jocius 2008).

Program Administration

By 2012, the UCBN I&M program is scheduled to be monitoring all 14 vital signs at full implementation. This increase in monitoring effort translates to an increased amount of scientific information that will need to be communicated to diverse audiences. Project leaders will produce monitoring protocols, develop status and trend reports, and annually write monitoring reports and update resource briefs. The UCBN currently employs one part-time science communications specialist (20 hours per week) who writes newspaper articles and press releases, develops lesson plans, updates and designs posters, updates the photo databases, and produces the bi-annual newsletter. It is anticipated that given the division of duties between project leaders, contractors, the network coordinator, data manager, and ecologists that a continued half-time position for a communication specialist will be necessary to maintain a robust science communication program.

Each year the UCBN will hire a qualified student from the University of Idaho who will work on the development of communication products for UCBN parks. The existing science and education partnership between the NPS and University of Idaho provides a solid foundation for this evolving program emphasis. Coursework related to interpretation may be required of interested applicants. Communication products developed by students will adhere to the following project criteria:

- Product(s) must facilitate connections between the target audience and the resources.
- Parks and residents within the Upper Columbia Basin region are the primary audience.
- Data must come primarily from the work of the I&M program.
- The communication product must highlight the work of the I&M program.
- The product(s) must be viable for at least one year.

Annual funding for a part-time student position for a science communication specialist will be placed in a task agreement each year with the University of Idaho. The UCBN Coordinator and University of Idaho Principal Investigator will jointly provide overall guidance for this employee. Potential communication products developed by this student are listed above under potential future communication products and tools. Project milestones will be coordinated with the academic year to provide the student with sufficient time to develop final communication products. The student will be asked to present information to park staff at park meetings when practical.

Additional consideration will be given to annual funding of an existing cooperative agreement between the UCBN and the Palouse-Clearwater Environmental Institute Americorps program. The UCBN used this agreement in 2006 and 2007 to develop a biodiversity interpretive handbook for CRMO and to assist NEPE staff in developing a curriculum for use in the educational component of the Camas Citizen Science Monitoring Program. This partnership is limited to park projects that take place in the state of Idaho.

Evaluation of the UCBN Science Communication Plan

How does an organization know if it is successful in communicating its messages? Evaluation is the only way to identify successes as well as potential failures in achieving the goals of a communication plan and to make appropriate changes. Once it is understood what works and what does not, messages and products can be tailored accordingly. Formative and summative evaluation techniques were used throughout the planning process. Formative evaluation occurs during the development of a program or product, and is explained for this plan below. Summative evaluation occurs at the end of a project to assess its success in meeting program goals.

Formative Evaluation
Formative evaluation was used during the development of this communication plan and provided early feedback so that improvements were incorporated into the final content. The goal of the formative evaluation phase was to detect ineffective strategies before beginning intensive efforts to complete development of the communication plan. Initial review of plan content was sought from park interpretive staff, resource managers, and superintendents, as well as UCBN scientific staff. This same strategy will be applied when developing new communication products such as podcasts or updated brochures.

Summative Evaluation
Summative evaluation is used to assess the success and failures of the UCBN communication program and to determine future needs for continuation or expansion of communication products. An overall evaluation is conducted annually at the Science Day meeting in October. UCBN staff query the Board of Directors and Science Advisory Committee members on whether the UCBN science communication program is meeting their needs. Other low-cost methods that will be used in the future to evaluate effectiveness will be to evaluate the number of hits to the UCBN website and to develop an annual email survey sent to NPS staff assessing UCBN communication products.

Literature Cited

Colorado State University (CSU) and NPS Office of Education and Outreach. 2007. HeartlandNetwork Inventory and Monitoring Program communication plan. [place of publication unknown].

Fancy, S.G., J.E. Gross, and S.L. Carter. 2009. Monitoring the condition of natural resources in US national parks. Environmental Monitoring and Assessment. 151: 161-174.

Garrett, L. K., T. J. Rodhouse, G. H. Dicus, C. C. Caudill, and M. R. Shardlow. 2007. Upper Columbia Basin Network vital signs monitoring plan. National Park Service, Fort Collins, CO: Natural Resource Report NPS/UCBN/NRR-2007/002.

HaySmith, L., and C. Nash. 2009. Pacific Island Network science communications strategies and plan, five year plan (2009-2014). Natural Resource Report NPS/PACN/NRR—2009/102. National Park Service, Fort Collins, Colorado.

Lewis, S. 2007. The George Wright Forum. The role of science in National Park Service decision-making. Retrieved February 2, 2009 from http://www.georgewright.org/242lewis.pdf.

Margoluis, R. and N. Salafsky. 1998. Measures of success: designing, managing, and monitoring conservation and development projects. Island Press, Washington, D.C.

National Park Service (NPS). 1999. Natural resource challenge: the National Park Service's action plan for preserving natural resources. US Department of the Interior National Park Service, Washington D.C. Online (http://www.nature.nps.gov/challengedoc.html). Accessed December 2008.

National Park Service (NPS) Education and Outreach. 2002. Four steps for effectively communicating natural resource topics and issues. User's guide from http://inside.nps.gov/programs/function.cfm?fun=173&div=34&prog=254&page=home (accessed January 2009).

National Park Service (NPS). 2003. Outline for vital signs monitoring plans. Integral guidance document. USDI National Park Service, Inventory and Monitoring Program, Ft. Collins, CO.

National Park Service. 2008. Component for Module 101, how interpretation works: the interpretive equation. Interpretive Development Program, professional standards for learning and performance. Online. (http://www.nps.gov/idp/interp/101/howitworks.htm). Accessed 24 April 2009.

National Park Service (NPS). 2009a. Nature and Science: The Inventory and Monitoring Program. Online. (http://science.nature.nps.gov/im/). Accessed 26 January 2009.

National Park Service (NPS). 2009b. Volunteer homepage. Online. (http://www.nps.gov/volunteer/). Accessed 23 February 2009.

Novey, L. 2007. A report on the communication needs and preferences for the Inventory and Monitoring program: Upper Columbia Basin Network. Unpublished report.

Novey, L., and J. Jocius. 2008. UCBN image database user guide (Jan. 2008 draft version): Upper Columbia Basin Network. Unpublished report.

Appendix A. Camas monitoring poster.

Appendix B. Winter/Spring 2009 UCBN newsletter *Basin Bulletin*.

Inventory and Monitoring

National Park Service
U.S. Department of Interior

Basin Bulletin
Volume 3, Issue 1
Winter/Spring 2009

In This Edition

Cover Story: Thoughts Afield, pg. 4	♫♪ The Age of Aquarius...♪ pg. 4	A Perspective on the NPS I&M Program, pg. 5
In the field with Wallace Keck, City of Rocks superintendent, and Eva Strand, aspen project leader.	Network Aquatic Technician, Eric Starkey, launches Aquarius Time Series™ software to analyze this year's water quality data. What an age to be in!	Gerry Wright, Retired NPS Research Scientist and Professor Emeritus, University of Idaho, offers his thoughts on implementing the vital signs monitoring program.

UPPER COLUMBIA
BASIN NETWORK
UCBN

PLUS!

- What's new on the UCBN website? Check out page 4 for details.
- Find out who won the UCBN photo contest on page 5.
- Devin Stucki, biotechnician, reflects on his first year working for the UCBN, page 6.
- We are proud to present a new "Featured Creature" on page 6. Can you pick out the *real* fairy shrimp?

Appendix B. Winter/Spring 2009 UCBN newsletter *Basin Bulletin* (continued).

National Park Service
U.S. Department of Interior
Upper Columbia Basin Network

The National Park Service has implemented natural resource inventory and monitoring on a servicewide basis to ensure all park units possess the resource information needed for effective, science-based managerial decision-making, and resource protection.

Upper Columbia Basin Network
University of Idaho
Department of Fish and Wildlife
Moscow, ID 83844-1136

Website
http://science.nature.nps.gov/im/units/ucbn

Network Coordinator
Lisa Garrett   (208) 885-3684
Lisa_Garrett@nps.gov

Network Ecologist
Tom Rodhouse   (541) 318-3726
Tom_Rodhouse@nps.gov

Network Data Manager/Ecologist
Gordon Dicus   (208) 885-3022
Gordon_Dicus@nps.gov

Network Biological Technician
Eric Starkey   (208) 885-3010
estarkey@uidaho.edu

Network Science Communicator
Jannis Jocius   (208) 885-3015
jannis_jocius@nps.gov

Newsletter Contributors
Wallace Keck,
Devin Stucki
Eric Starkey
Gerry Wright

Distribution
Please distribute this newsletter on to any person or group who is interested!
Questions about the newsletter?
Write to:
Jannis Jocius, Editor
jannis_jocius@nps.gov

The Coordinator's Corner

We wrapped up a busy fall season with writing and editing several annual reports, organizing the annual Science Day, and producing the Network annual report and work plan. The Network will be finishing up the aspen, sagebrush-steppe and water quality protocols in 2009 and drafting protocols for osprey and limber pine. Hopefully we will be adding an administrative support assistant and an aquatic biologist to our staff in 2009.

We would like to extend our gratitude to the parks of the UCBN for their continued staff and financial support in 2008. All of the parks contributed staff time to assist our program in various monitoring activities. We would like to especially thank Jason Lyon, at Nez Perce NHP, and Roger Trick, at Whitman Mission NHS, who were instrumental in assisting our water quality program leader, Eric Starkey, in field testing the water quality monitoring protocol this past year. A huge thanks to Doug Neighbor, superintendent at Craters of the Moon NM&P, who assisted the Network with the purchase of a pop-up camper for summer field crews working in Network parks. Jerald Weaver, from Lake Roosevelt NRA, donated funds for the purchase of GPS units and hard drives. Roger Trick arranged for the purchase of a Hydrolab multiprobe for collection of water quality data at Whitman Mission NHS. We would also like to recognize the support of Craig Dalby at the Pacific West Regional Office with the purchase of a Trimble GPS unit for the Network. Alyse Cadez, interpretive education specialist at Nez Perce National Historical Park, continues to take the lead with recruiting and training students to assist us in our annual camas monitoring effort. THANKS EVERYONE!!

We are launching several new initiatives this year that we hope will engage the parks in partnering with the Network to provide additional interpretive opportunities using inventory and monitoring information. The first project is utilizing the talent and expertise of Network interpreters in writing a com-

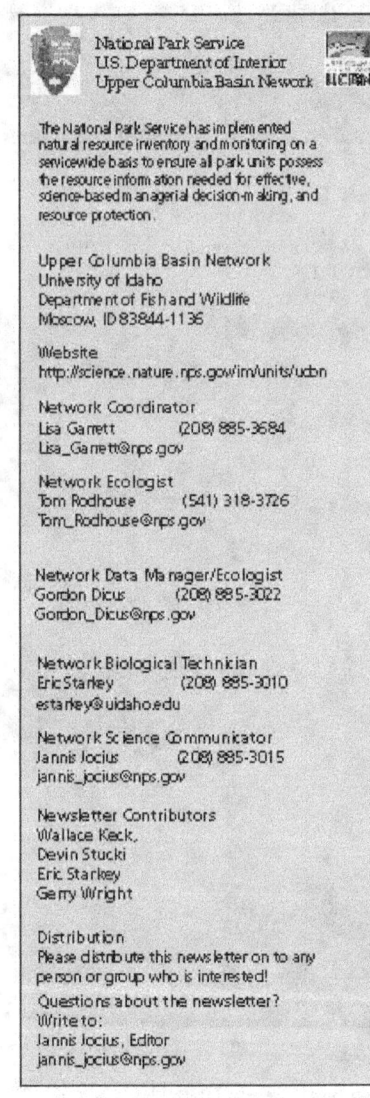

2008 Science Advisory Committee

munication plan. Jannis Jocius, the Network communication specialist, is taking the lead on this project and has contacted the park interpretive staff for their input. A second project that Jannis is working on is writing lesson plans to assist citizen scientists at LARO and NEPE in manipulating and analyzing data in GIS. We hope to have both the communication plan and GIS lesson plans ready for review by Network parks in early spring.

The field season will be upon us before you know it, although judging by the snow banks on my driveway it's hard to imagine. Northwest Management, Inc. and their field crews will be collecting vegetation plot data at City of Rocks National Reserve this summer. They will also be collecting on-site data for the natural resource condition assessment project for the southern parks. Network field crews will be collecting aspen, camas, osprey, sagebrush-steppe, and water quality monitoring data in parks this season. We look forward to another ambitious and productive year of monitoring natural resources in Upper Columbia Basin Network parks in 2009.

Lisa Garrett
UCBN Coordinator

52

Appendix B. Winter/Spring 2009 UCBN newsletter *Basin Bulletin* (continued).

UCBN Inventory and Monitoring Program Update January 2009

Project	Parks Included	Status
Aspen Monitoring	CIRO, CRMO	Data collection scheduled June 2009. Reporting scheduled for completion October 2009
Camas Monitoring	BIHO, NEPE	Data collection scheduled for May 2009 (NEPE) and June 2009 (BIHO). Reporting scheduled for completion October 2009
Natural Resource Condition Assessment	All UCBN Parks	Final report due for JODA, LARO, NEPE, and WHMI in February 2009. Field work begins for BIHO, CIRO, CRMO, and HAFO in May 2009
Osprey	LARO	Initial protocol development April 2009. Osprey monitoring data collection scheduled at LARO during June and July 2009
Pika	CRMO	Analysis, reporting, and close-out scheduled for completion by October 2009; Participation in 4-park NRPP project ongoing 2009
Photomonitoring (targeted projects)	NEPE, WHMI	Weippe Prairie photomonitoring May 2009 (NEPE). Doan Creek restoration photomonitoring project June 2009 (WHMI)
Integrated Riparian Monitoring	BIHO, CIRO, JODA, NEPE, WHMI	Initial protocol development July–August 2009
Sagebrush-steppe Vegetation Monitoring	CRMO, JODA, LARO	Revised protocol scheduled for completion March 2009 Field work scheduled from May – June 2009
Statistical Assistance	All UCBN parks	Multi-Network task agreement is funded for continued assistance in FY09
Vegetation Mapping	CIRO, CRMO, HAFO, JODA, LARO	CIRO – Vegetation plot data collection April-July 2009 CRMO – Completion report due HAFO – Completion report due JODA – Photo-interpretation planned LARO – Preliminary maps in progress
Water Quality Monitoring	BIHO, CIRO, WHMI	Water chemistry and macroinvertebrate data collection at BIHO and CIRO. Water chemistry data collection for Mill Creek (WHMI). Field work begins in late May-early June 2009

Appendix B. Winter/Spring 2009 UCBN newsletter *Basin Bulletin* (continued).

Thoughts Afield
Wallace Keck
Superintendent, City of Rocks National Reserve

Superintendent Keck, City of Rocks National Reserve

One of the benefits of superintending a small park is the opportunity I have to discover the site's intimate details as I venture afield and as the various inventory and monitoring studies cross my desk for review. On the other hand, one of the drawbacks to a small operation is the limited staff available to conduct all the science required to make sound management decisions. Fortunately, small parks in the Upper Columbia Basin Network have a team of professionals anxious and skilled to meet that need.

The UCBN's I&M partners and contractors have provided City of Rocks with a number of baseline studies including aspen and sagebrush steppe monitoring, bat inventories, natural resource condition assessments, and preliminary work on an integrated riparian program. These reports are not just pages of data. As land management progresses, we are able look at this data and see if we are fulfilling the mission of the Park Service. We can ask questions like, are the aspen stands regenerating or contracting; has the water quality improved through grazing management strategies, or do we need to alter practices; and, how do we maintain the health and diversity of the park's sagebrush-steppe?

It's one thing for this superintendent to boast about the superlatives of CIRO like the state's largest pinyon pine forest, or the presence of sage grouse leks. It's quite another to understand the status and trends of these. The I&M program is, essentially, taking CIRO's vital signs, and diagnosing the state of its health.

I appreciate that after weeks of working in an office, I can set that work aside for a few days when Lisa, Tom, Gordon, Eric, and the gang come to the "City." I can focus on the field issues that first lured me into this profession, and I can look for ways to bridge the gap between political gab and the language of the land. Finally, I appreciate that the UCBN team tolerates this botanist and birder, tagging along in the field, hoping to absorb some scientific acumen as the real work progresses.

This Just In!!
Gordon Dicus, UCBN Data Manager

Recent additions to the UCBN website include presentations from last fall's Science Advisory Committee (SAC) meeting and resource briefs from network inventory and monitoring projects. These downloadable files can be found by clicking the "What's New" link on the UCBN homepage. General updates to project information and downloadable files are ongoing. If you have any comments or questions regarding the UCBN website, please contact the network data manager at Gordon_Dicus@nps.gov.

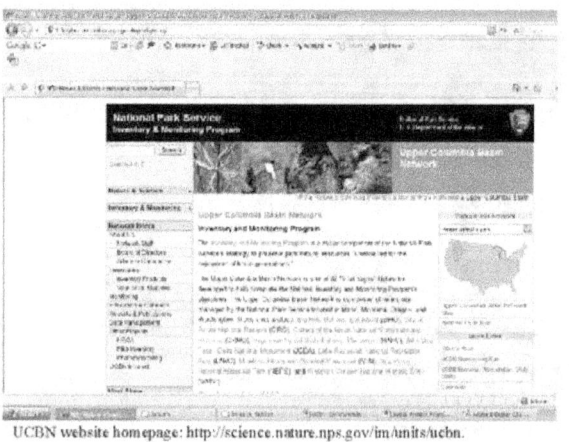

UCBN website homepage: http://science.nature.nps.gov/im/units/ucbn.

A Perspective on the NPS I&M
Gerry Wright
Retired NPS Research Scientist and Professor Emeritus, University of Idaho

Prior to the onset of the I&M Program, most National Park Service (NPS) units had limited data on the status of their biological resources, usually only the most common elements, and their trends over time were generally unknown. Furthermore, obtaining this data was often a low priority for park managers burdened by a variety of needs that were considered to be more pressing. The natural resource monitoring programs that did exist over the years were often short-lived, focused on the charismatic resources, and/or generally tied to the disciplinary interests of individual natural resource personnel. The end result was that natural resource problems were often not detected until it was too late and some resources were lost or at least impaired.

UCBN field team and National Oceanic and Atmospheric Administration (NOAA) taking measurements at John Day Fossil Beds National Monument.

I have long been an advocate of the need for parks to know and understand the status and trends of their natural resources. Thus, I was immensely gratified when the I&M Program was established and funded at a level commensurate with the need. Although I have never been a proponent of top-down programs, I believe the centralized organization of this program with its established protocols was necessary to assure its success.

The first priority of the NPS I&M Program was to do as thorough an inventory as possible of all of the biological resources in the parks. This inventory has been largely completed, and in my opinion the effort has been very successful. The resulting databases of natural resources are invaluable. The monitoring program now

in development or underway throughout the different networks is attempting to balance the need to use scientifically sound methodology while recognizing that the complexity, time commitment, and expense of the methods needs to be minimized. Whether these somewhat conflicting objectives can be met remains to be seen. Resource monitoring programs have historically suffered because their originators have had a desire to make them as all-inclusive as possible resulting in often complex and time-consuming methods. This typically made them short-lived because the time, money, and interest in continuing them over time often waned. Some of the monitoring protocols developed by different networks appear to me to suffer from this problem. Whether they will be successful over time is therefore an open question.

All of the monitoring programs are intended to focus on key natural resources or processes, known as vital signs, contained in the parks within a given network. In my opinion, the process used to select these vital signs was overly elaborate, complex, expensive, and time-consuming. This criticism seems particularly apparent in hindsight as the list of vital signs produced by each network seems remarkably intuitive to individuals familiar with the resources of the respective parks in a network. It is also apparent in the fact that across the system, many networks share similar vital signs in common.

A large effort that has been expended by the various networks to develop and test monitoring protocols; probably a greater effort than was necessary. And while there has been some sharing of protocols among networks, this could have been expanded, particularly since the vital signs of many networks are similar. I am firmly convinced that for the I&M Program to succeed over the long term, all of the monitoring protocols used need to be as simple, cost effective, and automated as possible. This will allow data collection to begin as soon as possible, which is, after all, the goal of the program. Without these emphases, given this history of shifts in natural resource policy in the NPS, there is a real danger that the program could collapse under its own weight and/or funding reduced. I sincerely hope this will not be the case.

University of Idaho

Appendix B. Winter/Spring 2009 UCBN newsletter *Basin Bulletin* (continued).

This past field season has just come to an end, and I'm already looking forward to the next. I'm a student at Central Oregon Community College in Bend, working toward a Bachelor's degree in Botany. This upcoming field season will be my second with the National Park Service's Inventory and Monitoring Program as a STEP hire. This has provided an amazing opportunity to gain firsthand experience in my field of study, as well as with other projects.

The Inventory and Monitoring Program was developed to determine what natural resources are in parks and their status and distributions. With this baseline information, comparisons will be made with future studies to see how these parks are changing. This is a very important step toward promoting the health and diversity of the lands under the protection of the National Park Service and I'm glad to be a part of it.

The 2008 field crew was headed up by Tom Rodhouse and included Jim Bylund and myself. We worked closely with Dr. Jeff Yeo on sagebrush steppe vegetation monitoring and, gathered data with many other knowledgeable and dedicated people, including other park staff and volunteers from the Oregon Museum of Science and Industry (OMSI).

Field technicians, Jim Bylund and Devin Stucki, at Weippe Praire, Nez Perce National Historical Park during camas monitoring.

While most of our time was spent sampling steppe vegetation, we were also involved in monitoring aspen stands, counting camas plants, searching for pika, and setting up audio detectors for bats.

This past season was filled with excitement and challenges. There were always new problems to be solved, usually without delay. Fieldwork poses unique challenges because it is usually done in remote locations. Because of this, it is extremely important to be outfitted with the right equipment, to be prepared for any type of weather, and to have a detailed plan. I learned this without question this season. With plans for next season already underway, I'm anxious for the excitement to begin again.

-Devin Stucki
2008 Field Technician

#1 Badger (CRMO) Doug Owen

#2 Lava Tube (CRMO) Noel Jensen

#3 Rainbow Landscape (CJRO) Eric Starkey

Congratulations, winners of the 2008 UCBN Photo Contest!

Appendix B. Winter/Spring 2009 UCBN newsletter *Basin Bulletin* (continued).

♫♪The Age of Aquarius...Aquarius♫♪

Eric Starkey
Network Aquatic Technician

Now that you have a tune in your head...the UCBN has entered the age of Aquarius Time Series™ software. In the spring of 2008 the UCBN investigated the possibility of using Aquarius software to manage our continuouswater quality data. By late July, with financial assistance from the NPS-Water Resource Division, the UCBN purchased and began to pilot test this program for 31 other I&M networks.

The instrument we use to collect water quality data is called a Hydrolab. The hydrolab instrument records a reading for temperature, specific conductance, pH, dissolved oxygen, and turbidity once an hour for an entire month. The result is 720 samples per core parameter per month. At the end of each month, the instrument is re-calibrated and deployed for another month (May-October). At the end of the field season in October we have 4,300 hourly samples per core parameter. The sheer volume of data processing would have been extremely difficult without the use of this relatively new software.

After returning to the office with data from the previous month and measures of sensor drift and fouling, an entire 30 days or more of data (all 5 parameters) can be processed in just over an hour.

Aquarius Time Series Software allows us to graph our raw data, trim outliers, correct for fouling and drift, apply data quality ratings (grades), track corrections and grading, graph corrected data, run basic statistics, and much more! The software fits nicely with the integrated water quality protocol since we are using many standard United States Geological Survey practices for data correction and grading. Aquarius will allow us to efficiently operate multiple Hydrolabs and assess water quality within hours after a monthly site visit.

The UCBN would like to extend our sincere thanks to the Water Resource Division for providing the necessary funding to the Network to purchase Aquarius Time Series software. We look forward to reporting additional results of our pilot testing efforts at the George Wright Society Meeting in Portland, Oregon in March 2009.

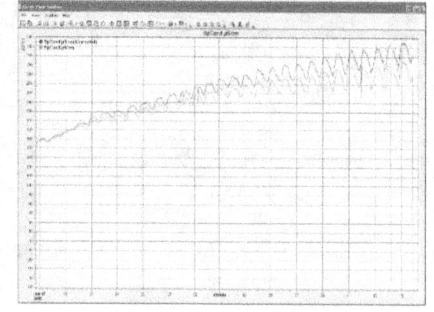

Highlights of Aquarius: Data correction for fouling and drift.

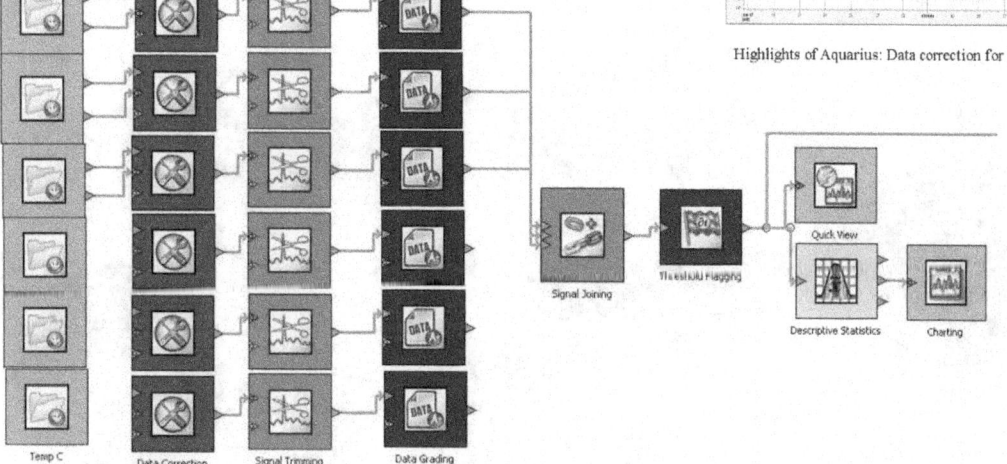

Aquarius' unique whiteboard workspace.

"Featured Creature"
Shrimp on the Rocks
By Eric Starkey

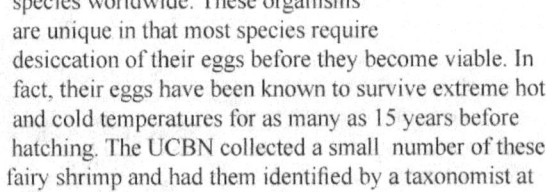

As the UCBN conducted sagebrush steppe monitoring in City of Rocks National Reserve Devin Stucki discovered several new vernal pools. A vernal pool is an ephemeral pool of water drying out at least once a year that may contain invertebrate life. After further investigation the UCBN crew discovered these pools were teaming with fairy shrimp. Fairy shrimp are a very robust group of freshwater crustaceans containing over 200 species worldwide. These organisms are unique in that most species require desiccation of their eggs before they become viable. In fact, their eggs have been known to survive extreme hot and cold temperatures for as many as 15 years before hatching. The UCBN collected a small number of these fairy shrimp and had them identified by a taxonomist at

Devin Stucki collecting fairy shrimp(*Branchinecta constricta*) samples at City of Rocks National Preserve.

Eco-Analysts in Davis, CA. When the results were in, the UCBN had collected *Branchinecta constricta* Rogers, 2006. To much surprise, this discovery represented a significant range extension of this species which was originally described from the east side of the Continental Divide in Wyoming. As the UCBN continues monitoring efforts in City of Rocks National Reserve we plan on investigating other vernal pools to check on the status of these shrimp and see what other discoveries may lay amongst the rocks.

Can you guess which of these is the real fairy shrimp?

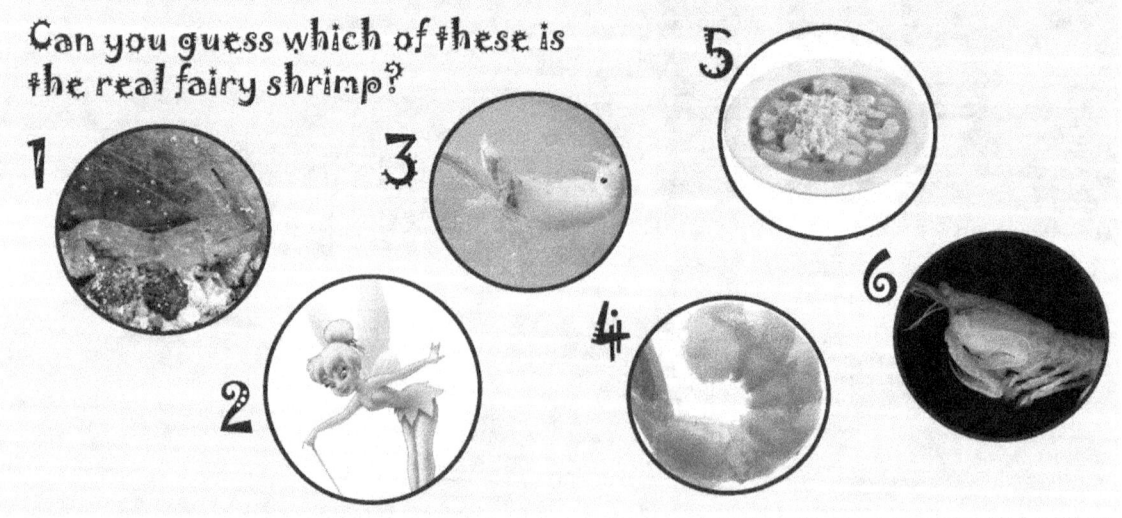

Answers: 1: Mantis shrimp (from the stomatopoda family). 2: Disney's fairy, Tinkerbell 3: Fairy shrimp (*branchinecta lynchi*) 4. Frozen shrimp for cocktails. 5: Shrimp gumbo, yummy! 6: Pistol shrimp, also called snapping or symbiosis shrimp (*Alpheus bellulus*).

Appendix C. Water quality resource brief (WHMI).

Upper Columbia Basin Network
Resource Brief

Inventory & Monitoring
National Park Service
U.S. Department of the Interior

Water Quality Monitoring at Whitman Mission National Historical Site (WHMI)

Importance

Freshwater habitats are diverse and productive ecosystems, providing habitat for aquatic plant, invertebrate, and vertebrate species including many fishes and birds. Rivers and streams are intimately connected to riparian zones, providing habitat for many specialist species. Additionally, most upland animals rely on aquatic habitats to one degree or another. Water resources in the semi-arid west have been strongly affected by human acitvity, and all UCBN streams and rivers are listed by states as impaired for one or more parameters. Most UCBN waterbodies and many aquatic resources such as migratory fish are strongly influenced by activities in the larger watersheds outside park boundaries. Understanding the current status of freshwater ecosystems will help guide management and restoration efforts and provide insight into ecosystem change in a landscape with changing climate and dynamic human influences.

WHMI resource manager calibrating the continuous water quality monitor.

Status at Whitman Mission National Historical Site (WHMI)

Threats to water resources in WHMI have been identified as: agricultural chemical use, over allocation of irrigation water, and a private airfield 3 miles upstream. In 2002 and 2004 Doan Creek exceeded the state Department of Environmental Quality (DEQ) criteria for temperature. As a result Washington DEQ designates Doan Creek as a category 5 waterbody and lists the creek as impaired on the EPA 303(d) list. In 2004 Mill Creek was listed as 303(d) impaired for dissolved oxygen, pH, temperature, and fecal coliform. Consequently Mill Creek is also listed as a Category 5 (303d) stream by Washington DEQ.

In 2008 the UCBN monitored 5 core water chemistry parameters in Mill Creek including: dissolved oxygen, pH, specific conductance, temperature, and turbidity. Each parameter was evaluated hourly between the months of June and November using a continuous water quality monitor. In addition, aquatic macroinvertebrates were collected from Mill Creek using the EPA's EMAP protocol. For more information on macroinvertebrates in Mill Creek please see the integrated water quality annual report for WHMI on the UCBN website listed below. Monitoring of Doan Creek was limited in 2008 due to restoration efforts and low water conditions.

Mill Creek Water Chemistry Summary 2008

Measure	Current Condition (June-October, 2008)	State DEQ Thresholds
Temperature (MDMT, MDAT)	MDMT= 25.47 °C MDAT= 22.92 °C °C	7-DADMax <13 °C
Specific Conductance (mean)	287.70 µS/cm	N/A
Dissolved oxygen (min. daily min.)	3.73 mg/L	>5.0 mg/L Minimum Daily Minimum
pH (mean daily max)	8.89 pH Units	8.5 pH Units, Max
pH (mean daily min)	7.65 pH Units	6.0 pH Units, Min
Turbidity (mean daily max)	5.97 NTU	< 5 NTU increase above background when background NTU < 50, < 10% increase when background NTU > 50

7-DADMax –7 DayAverage Daily Maximum Temperature

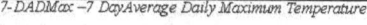

MDMT – Maximum Daily Maximum Temperature, MDAT – Maximum Daily Average Temperature

Mill Creek, WHMI, WA

Discussion

Sub-optimal temperatures, dissolved oxygen, and pH indicate impaired conditions in Mill Creek. Also of concern is the dewatering of Mill and Doan Creeks due to irrigation. Improving water quality within WHMI will depend on riparian and water use improvements basin wide. For this reason cooperation with other agencies and stakeholders will be critical. Future monitoring efforts will include more intensive efforts on Doan Creek to help evaluate restoration efforts. UCBN water quality monitoring is conducted on a 3 year rotating panel. Mill and Doan Creeks will be sampled for water chemistry and macroinvertebrates again in 2011.

Contact Information

Eric Starkey, estarkey@uidaho.edu

Network website: http://science.nature.nps.gov/im/units/ucbn/
Resource website: http://science.nature.nps.gov/im/units/ucbn/monitor/waterquality/waterquality.cfm

January 2009

Appendix C. Water quality resource brief (WHMI) (continued).

Upper Columbia Basin Network
Resource Brief

Inventory & Monitoring
National Park Service
U.S. Department of the Interior

Monitoring Data for Whitman Mission National Historical Site (WHMI), 2008

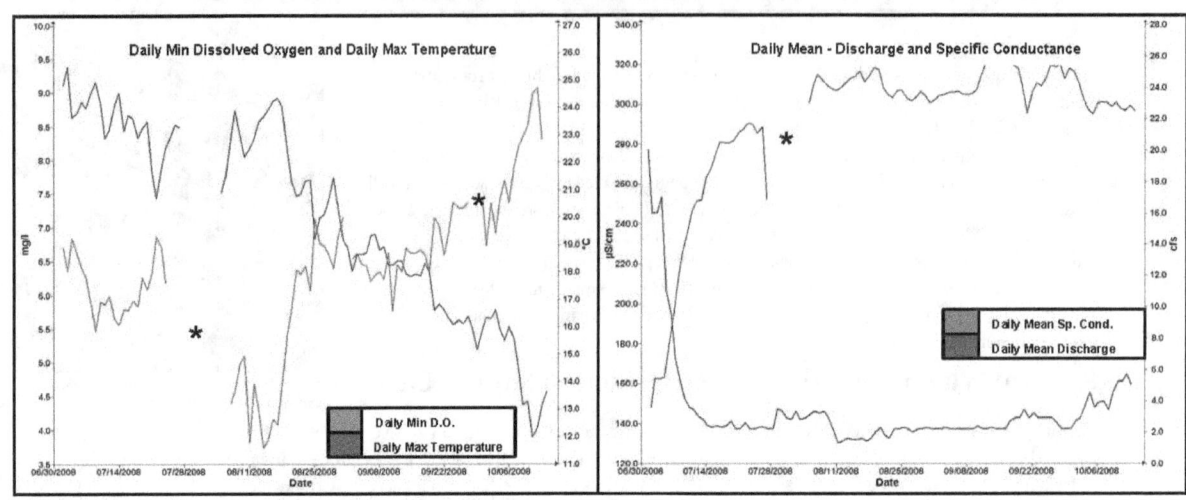

Note that temperature exceeded the regulatory threshold daily maximum of 20 °C a total of 51 days. Daily minimum dissolved oxygen was below the recommended threshold (5.0 mg/L) on 12 days.

The mean specific conductance was 287.70 µS/cm. There is no established threshold for specific conductance. The inverse relationship between discharge and specific conductance is typical for streams. Note that discharge in Mill Creek is highly regulated for irrigation.

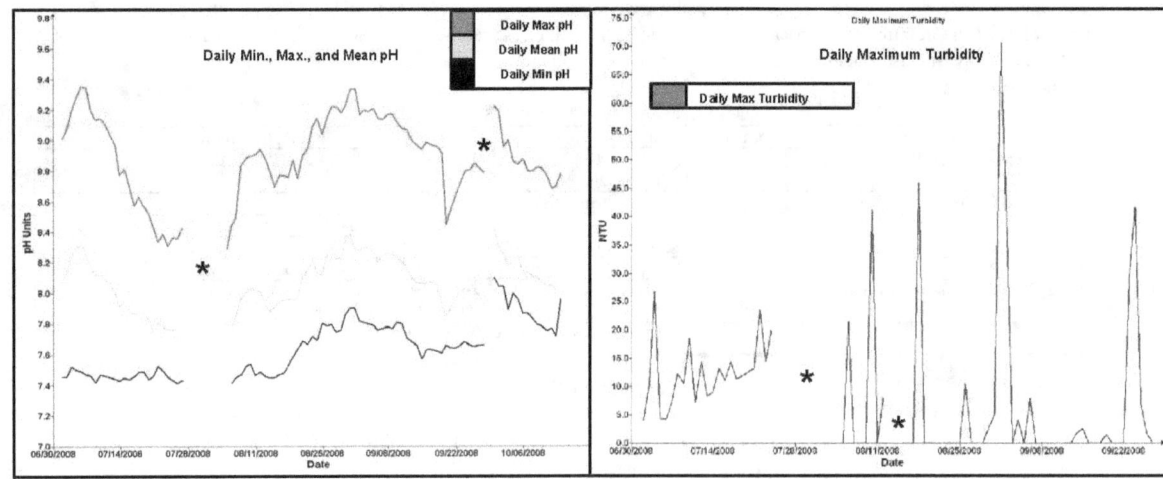

The regulatory threshold for Mill Creek is between 6.0 and 8.5 pH units. pH was never below 6.0 while pH exceeded 8.5 a total of 84 days. Mean pH was 8.08.

Daily maximum turbidity ranged from near 0 NTU to 71 NTU. Spikes in turbidity should be viewed with some caution as fouling likely contributed to these spikes. Instantaneous turbidity values occasionally exceeded threshold criteria but were likely caused by fouling or low battery power and are not of concern. Note missing data from 9/22 until the end of season due to sensor malfunction.

Important Notes:

*Indicates a break in data due to service dates and/or a loss of battery power.

All data has been corrected for fouling and drift error according to guidelines established by the USGS.

January 2009

Appendix D. Informational poster on pika (CRMO).

Inventory and Monitoring
National Park Service
U.S. Department of the Interior

UPPER COLUMBIA BASIN NETWORK
UCBN

A Tail-less Tale:
Searching for Furry Little Creatures...

Scientists will be Collecting Pika Data in the Park this Week

Pika (Ochotona princeps)

The National Park Service is monitoring pika as a key natural resource at this park so that resource managers can make important management decisions based on sound scientific information. "Vital Signs" monitoring is an integral part of a park's adaptive management program because it provides critical information about status and trends in natural resource conditions.

Evidence of pika: piles of edible grasses and shrub clippings.

Fresh pika scat on a lava rock.

Searching for signs of pika in lava rock cracks and crevices.

Did you know pikas...
- might be at a risk of extinction given the current predictions of climate change over the next century? (Beever et al. 2003, Wagner et al., 2003, Grayson 2005, Parmesan 2006)
- do not hibernate? Instead they "thermoregulate" which means that they keep their body temperatures within certain boundaries, even when the temperature surrounding them is very different.
- commonly make peculiar short squeaks while sitting atop rocks?
- store grasses and herbs in "haypiles" as food storage?
- live where few people ever go? (Burt et al. 1980)
- don't have any visible tails?!
- are part of the rabbit family?
- like to make their homes in rockslides and in rocky crevices?

A pika hunched on a rock at Craters of the Moon National Monument and Preserve.

Contact Information
Tom_Rodhouse@nps.gov

For more information about the vital signs that the National Park Service will be monitoring, research findings, and contact information, please visit our Network website at:
http://www.nature.nps.gov/im/units/ucbn

61

Appendix E. List of recipients of version 1.0 of the UCBN Science Communication Plan.

Park	Superintendent	Resource Manager	Chief of Interpretation/Specialist	Education Specialist/Other
BIHO	Steve Black	Jimmer Stevenson	Mandi Wick	
CIRO	Wallace Keck	Jay Goodwin		
CRMO	Doug Neighbor	John Apel	Ted Stout	
HAFO	Wendy Janssen	Mike Wissenbach	Annette Rousseau	
JODA	Jim Hammett	Shirley Hoh	John Fiedor	
LARO	Debbie Bird	Jerald Weaver	Lee Snook	Janice Elvidge
NEPE	Gary Somers	Jason Lyon	Terry O'Halloran	Marc Blackburn; Alyse Cadez
WHMI	Terry Darby	Roger Trick	Roger Trick	Mike Dedman

The Department of the Interior protects and manages the nation's natural resources and cultural heritage; provides scientific and other information about those resources; and honors its special responsibilities to American Indians, Alaska Natives, and affiliated Island Communities.

NPS 963/100250, August 2009

www.ingramcontent.com/pod-product-compliance
Lightning Source LLC
Chambersburg PA
CBHW081558170526
45166CB00009B/2743